Minnesota ℭ

by Joan Claire Graham
and
33 Friends

Here is a sure-fire recipe for fun: Get together with a couple of old friends, and take turns reading this book aloud. _Minnesota Memories_ stories trigger free-association, and that is where the fun comes in. People start listening to a story--often sitting with arms crossed in front of their chests. As the stories and characters unfold, however, they loosen up, lean forward, and begin to nod and smile. Chuckles ensue.

Afterwards, people start to tell their own stories about their town characters or their teen hangouts or their favorite teacher. And they always seem to have a good time because memories are a done deal.

With so many crazy things going on in today's world, we can take comfort in stories about the past. Unlike our current worries and concerns, these stories have already turned out the way they're going to turn out. Good or bad--memories can be reinterpreted, but they're beyond fixing, and there's no dramatic tension. Time has sanded off most rough edges, giving memories an impressionistic quality that renders them comfortable.

This is a collection of stories about real, not fictional, people, places, experiences, and events. Tones range from hilarious to tragic. Writers lived in places like Albert Lea, Baudette, Mankato, South St. Paul, Hallock, International Falls, Litchfield, Clinton, Robbinsdale, Winona, and Beroun.

These are forty-eight extraordinary stories from thirty-four ordinary folks. Although many stories in this collection are about as funny as any you'll ever read, writers do not caricature or make fun of those experiences, people, and customs we hold dear. There are no hotdish jokes or stories about Ole and Lena. These stories ring true because they honestly reflect our collective memory of life in the North Star State. And those reflections need no exaggeration or embellishment in order to be as good as they really are. _For Deanna — Jean Claire Graham_

Story Contributors

Name	Town	Page
1 Frances J. Arenz	Winona	103
2 Marilyn Mikulewicz Baranski	Hastings	145, 149
3 Mary Bongard	South St. Paul	175
4 Carol Adair Brune	Baudette	180
5 David J. Chrz	Austin	127, 129
6 Betty Jean Rueckert Collins	Minnesota Lake, Wells	172
7 Eleanore Davidson	Rushford	108
8 Lloyd Deuel	Foreston	59
9 Esther Henderson Eaton	Beroun, Pine City	50
10 Florence Edwardson	Lanesboro	110
11 Madonna Erkenbrack	International Falls	140
12 Graham Frear	Minnetonka Mills	152, 157
13 Richard Hall	Austin, Aitkin County	132
14 Vernon Johnson	Lake Bronson	95, 99
15 Julie Westrum King	Albert Lea	112
16 Tom Kropidlowski	Winona	106
17 Clayton Lagerquist	Mankato	54
18 Bernice Lanik	Winona	100
19 Jon Lynott	Ely & Duluth	166
20 Don Matecjeck	Owatonna	116
21 Kathy Megyeri	Owatonna	119, 123
22 Jennifer Laura Paige	Minneapolis	183
23 Governor Tim Pawlenty	St. Paul	188
24 Edward John Peterson	Lindstrom	68
25 Ed Putzier	Litchfield, Greenleaf	170, 172
26 Sister Mary Lonan Reilly	Winona	76
27 Arvin Rolfs	Kenneth, Luverne	142
28 Patricia Ryan	Inver Grove Heights	164
29 Alice Stielow	Graceville, Clinton	159
30 Steve Swanson	Northfield	79, 81
31 Tom Veblen	Hallock	83, 90
32 Dexter Westrum	Albert Lea	73
33 Rosemary Wulff	Rochester	85
34 Joan Claire Graham	Albert Lea, Robbinsdale, Mankato	5-49

Cover Photo: Lake Ely, by Aquinata " Cookie" Graham. Thanks, Mom.

Back Cover Photo by Leah Nell Peterson, Cannon Falls Beacon

Minnesota Memories 3 Copyright 2003

Graham Megyeri Books--Minnmemory@aol.com

ISBN 0-9711971-2-1

Minnesota Memories 3
Table of Contents

Special thanks to the following: Laura Resler at Steel County Historical Society, Cindy Adams and Marcy Johnson at Kitteson County Historical Society, Walter Bennick at Winona County Historical Society, Terry Cole. Cindy Stewart at Kittson County Enterprise, Pavek Museum of Broadcasting, *Keeping Carnies Honest: A Police Officer's field Guide to Carnival Game Inspections* by Lindsay Smith and Bruce Walstad, George Lanik, Kathy Megyeri, Minnesota Department of Tourism, Colgate Palmolive and all the real--not fictional--Minnesota people who made these stories memorable.

Say Something
by Joan Claire Graham

I had a long and amusing conversation with a story contributor last year about the strange ability of some Minnesota people to speak volumes by practicing the art of saying nothing. I remember my mother telling me when something went wrong or someone shortchanged me, "Don't *say anything,* because that will only make trouble." When she really got frustrated, she would relate an annoying incident and add, "I got so mad I almost *said something."*

People I knew believed that any person you were thinking of saying something to had psychic powers to discern what was wrong, that he knew what your complaint would be, and that he would correct the problem to your satisfaction on his own time and in his own way. If you spoke words of complaint, however, your words might hurt his feelings and cause an irreparable rift--even if your complaint was legitimate or if it appeared obvious that the complainee had committed an oversight. The amazing truth is that sometimes this technique worked.

If your neighbor's dog was barking late at night, for example, you would not say anything. Your neighbor would know how put out you were if you just gave him the silent treatment and said nothing, and if you waited patiently, he would eventually get rid of the dog. It might take ten or twelve years, but the barking would eventually stop. If the lady who hired you to babysit her kids from dawn till dark came home and paid you a measly two dollars, you would not say anything because doing so would embarrass both of you, and the tightwad mama might never speak to you again. But if you practiced restraint, she might actually overpay you sometime in the future. Saying something was a mark of ill breeding.

Without a doubt, the frustration and pent up hostility endured by practitioners of this *say nothing* philosophy prevented a few spats that might have developed between neighbors and relatives if something had been said. Some would say this was a pretty good trade-off. However, like any practice, saying nothing could be carried too far. Nothing exemplifies what I mean more than an incident that happened when my dad and his second wife Helen came to visit me in Robbinsdale in the late 70's.

My dad hated to venture from home because he always feared that adverse weather conditions would arise or an emergency would come up and prevent him from ever returning to his beloved house in Albert Lea. I guess he must have read and been deeply influenced by Homer's epic *The Odyssey* when he was at an impressionable age. Seventy years of life in Minnesota had not calmed his anxiety or taught him that no weather front stays in one place forever or that there were no cyclopes or sirens trying to prevent him from getting home to his beloved bed and LaZboy lounger. His usual plan for coping with his phobia was to arrive early, stay briefly, and leave soon.

His escape plan went awry, however, one year when he came for Christmas dinner. He got stuck at my house because of a combination of two unfortunate factors: 1. Dinner was delayed because my electric stove was not heating correctly. 2. While he waited to eat, the snow storm he had been eluding all his life finally caught up with him. His worst fear became reality. Precipitation was falling from the sky, and he had not yet returned to the safety and comfort of his own home. Not wanting to risk driving in snow a hundred miles down I35, Dad and Helen agreed to accept my invitation to sleep over.

Our house wasn't exactly a B&B, but if the need arose, we could accommodate a couple of overnight guests. On the sun porch adjacent to the living room, I kept my hide-a-bed made up at all times. The porch was cold in winter because it had ten windows, but if I opened the heat register out there and if sleepers were willing to keep the double glass doors to the living room open, the porch would stay warm enough for two people under blankets. Since Dad and Helen were still newlyweds, I was pretty sure they could manage to stay warm.

Helen decided to conk out around 9 p.m., which was a little early for the rest of us. I asked her if she wanted me to help her pull out the bed, but she preferred to ask my dad for help. I gave her a night gown and told her that she would find all the sheets, pillows and blankets she or anyone would ever need folded up in the bed. I even threw in the afghan from the living room couch for good measure. She went to bed without a word after my dad opened the bed. About an hour later, my dad started yawning, so the rest of us toddled off to give them a little privacy.

The next morning, I crept downstairs in the dark to start brewing coffee because I figured my dad would want to make a break for home as early as possible. The first unusual thing I noticed was that the sheepskin throw I kept on my rocking chair was missing. Going further, I saw that the dining room table cloth, the runner from the piano bench, the throw rug in front of the door and the Christmas tree skirt were also gone. Opening the coat closet, I was surprised to see that almost all the coats were missing. "Gosh," I thought, "have we been burgled?"

Noticing that the guests had ignored my advice and had shut the sun porch doors tightly, I cautiously took a peek through their curtain-covered glass windows. Because of the street light outside my house, I could clearly see a big heap of rugs, coats, skins, and tablecloths covering the sleeping couple.

At that point I had an awful recollection. Oh no, the last person to use my hide-a-bed had been my niece Erin. She had gotten a nosebleed, and I had to remove all the sheets, pillow cases and blankets so that I could get the stains out. The clean bedding had been sitting in a basket down the basement for about three months. I hadn't gotten around to putting it back on the bed because I didn't expect any company, and amidst Christmas preparations, I had forgotten all about it.

Realizing my mistake, I felt too embarrassed for words. I pictured my dad stealing around the house in the dark all night in his underpants, gathering table linen and animal pelts, and shutting the sun porch doors to the cats because he didn't want to sleep with any live animal pelts. I imagined Helen saying, " No Bert, I'm still cold. Go take the coats out of the closet. How about the Christmas tree skirt? Do they have any dish towels? And whatever you do, keep those cats out of here."

I pictured Helen telling Dad that I had distinctly told her that my hide-a-bed contained all the bedding any person would ever need. She must have thought I was nuts. No blankets! No Sheets! Nothing but a mattress pad! What kind of person was I? Did I grow up in a barn?

But why hadn't Helen said something when she went to bed early and noticed there were no sheets, blankets or pillow cases? Why hadn't my dad said something when he helped her unfold the hide-a-bed? A simple, " Hey, I thought you said there would be sheets and blankets," would have done the trick. I wouldn't have thought less of them if they had said something. I would have thought more of them!

When they awoke, I explained my snafu to my dad and Helen, but they merely assured me that everything had been just fine. No, they said, they weren't the least bit cold. Right. When was the last time anyone you knew used a Christmas tree skirt and coats to cover themselves because they were already warm enough?   Dad and Helen denied there had been a problem in the same strained tone of voice people use when they tell you they like your unattractive new hairdo.   There they sat, saying nothing, and I took absolutely no comfort in their frosty reserve.

That was the last time my dad and Helen ever stayed at my house. I'd invite them, and even try to cajole and tease them a bit. " Come on up for the weekend. I'll even throw in sheets and blankets this time." But they never took the bait. One time they stayed at a motel near my house; that's as close as they came.

Eventually I got to the point where I couldn't tell this story without laughing myself sick. It was just so funny to think of them traipsing through the dark gathering rugs and tablecloths. I guess we all lived to tell the tale, but the lesson I learned is that we Minnesotans should think about refining that old *say nothing* rule.

We shouldn't take our changes too far though. We need to preserve our reputation as nice people.   Minnesotans should not turn into New Yorkers who shout at taxi drivers, but we definitely need to clean up our *say nothing* act, especially when saying something becomes a matter of survival.   So I propose that we modify the *say nothing* rule to state that even well-bred people should be expected to say something in the following three circumstances: 1. If someone is standing on our foot, 2. If we are starving   3. If we are freezing on a blanketless hide-a-bed in a sun porch on a snowy Christmas night.   This small modification to the *say nothing* rule makes sense, and its implementation will not compromise our Minnesota nice reputations.

Remembering Eddie Cochran
by Joan Claire Graham

I was sitting in my turquoise vinyl swivel chair one Sunday evening in April, 1960, listening to my transistor radio and putting the finishing touches on a school assignment when I heard the news that Eddie Cochran had died in a car accident near London. I closed my bedroom door and cried quietly so that nobody would notice and tease me or tell me to stop.

The next day I cut out the *Albert Lea Tribune* article and stuck it in my Rock and Roll scrapbook. It ran on page one-- an objective news story with no photo or quotes from town residents who knew Eddie. Although he was a famous local boy who had moved away only seven years before his death, nobody attempted to turn this article into the kind of human interest story only a hometown newspaper could write. It wasn't that the editors were tired of eulogizing local celebrities; it was that they just didn't understand Eddie's importance. They belonged to a generation who hoped rock and roll would fade quickly so that the sounds of Tin Pan Alley could resume their popularity.

As an "American Bandstand" aficionado and fan of just about everything pop culture had to offer, I thought it was incredibly neat that the guy who sang "Summertime Blues" and " Sittin' in the Balcony" was born and raised in Albert Lea. I bought his records and looked through fan magazines down at Kieffers for photos and articles about Eddie. It was much easier to find articles about Pat Boone, Elvis Presley and Ricky Nelson. They must have had better publicists.

Throughout the years, whenever I needed to further define or defend my hometown, I'd describe its location near the Iowa border and add, "Hometown of Marion Ross, of ' Happy Days,' Richard Carlson of ' I Led Three Lives,' and Eddie Cochran. My little recitation would usually be followed by a beat....then a question, " Eddie Cochran?"

"You know---- 'There ain't no cure for the summertime blues,'" I'd sing. Nods followed, but I could tell they thought Eddie had been a one hit wonder. It didn't matter where he had grown up. As the years passed, I often wondered why Albert Lea didn't pay more attention to their local celebrity extraordinaire, and I listened whenever Eddie Cochran's name came up in discussions about rock and roll pioneers.

A few years ago, I saw Paul McCartney play "Twenty Flight Rock" on a television interview while explaining how he and George Harrison had been profoundly influenced when Eddie Cochran and Gene Vincent toured England just before the fatal crash. McCartney explained how rocker wannabes followed that tour from town to town, learning Eddie's innovative guitar riffs and finding inspiration in his clever lyrics, his sense of humor, and his stage persona. In fact, he said, when he met John Lennon, Paul impressed him by playing and singing all the verses to Cochran's "Twenty Flight Rock."

Turning from the television interview, I proudly said to my daughter, "Eddie Cochran was from Albert Lea," and she looked incredulous as I assured her that I was not kidding. How could a guy from Albert Lea, the sleepy little home of Grandma and Grandpa, inspire a musical legend like Paul McCartney? And if Eddie Cochran was such a big deal, why hadn't we heard about him when we visited Albert Lea?

For many years, the town that gave Eddie Cochran his foundation of values and his formative education chose to ignore him. After the Rock and Roll Hall of Fame inducted Eddie in 1987, his old friends decided the time had come for his hometown to take credit and pay homage.

Albert Lea did not have a town festival like most neighboring towns, so organizing one to honor Eddie Cochran seemed like a task waiting to be performed. His old friends and neighbors formed ECHO, the Eddie Cochran Historical Organization, and put together the first Eddie Cochran Days in 1991. Eddie's backup band, the Kelly Four, Richie Valens' brother Ernie and The Crickets performed, along with a local group called the Sidewalls. Eddie's mom and siblings attended, and the successful event attracted interest of fans across the country.

After some retooling, the Low Bucks Car Club took over organizing Eddie Cochran Days, a three-day trip back to the 50's that includes music, a street dance, a vintage car show, a flea market, and a memorial service at the historical society chapel. The festival takes place the second weekend of every June, and people from all over the world attend, including Eddie's family. Visitors who find themselves in Albert Lea at other times of the year can enjoy a permanent Eddie Cochran exhibit at The Freeborn County Historical Society Museum. Amidst photos, costumes, and memorabilia, a copy of his birth certificate proves to the skeptical that this kid was indeed born in Albert Lea.

In July of 2002, as I gathered my belongings to leave Albert Lea's KATE radio station after an interview, the receptionist handed me the telephone and said that a listener wanted to talk to me. The listener, Terry Cole, invited me to come to his house to talk about his old friend Eddie Cochran. Terry and Eddie were childhood pals, and he has remained friends with the Cochran family. Terry Cole's invitation seemed like too great an opportunity for the purveyor of memories to pass up, so on the following Sunday afternoon, my daughter and I paid him a visit.

I decided it would be interesting to listen to some Cochran music on our two-hour trip from Bloomington down I35 so I stopped at a Barnes and Noble that had a small music department. Almost apologetically I asked the clerk if they might possibly stock just something--maybe an oldies collection--with at least one cut by Eddie Cochran. I was surprised when she promptly turned around, reached up to a prominent display, and plunked down on the counter a CD containing twenty Eddie Cochran songs.

As we headed toward Albert Lea, we were amazed by the quantity, quality, and variety of Eddie's recorded work. Not all songs were great, but they were all interesting. Some of the vocals and arrangements sounded a little like Elvis, others like Little Richard, and others had a unique Eddie Cochran sound that other guys tried to imitate later. I had not heard most songs, and my daughter had only heard " Summertime Blues." Neither of us ejected the disk when the last track ended so we opted for a complete 20 track encore. Before we reached Albert Lea, we were keenly interested in finding out more about the wunderkind who came up with all this rock and roll music back in the mid to late 50's.

Terry Cole greeted us outside his comfortable south side house and eagerly ushered us inside so that he could share all he knows. He showed us framed photos of himself and Eddie in their snowsuits back in the 1940's. He proudly displayed more recent photos of himself among musicians and friends who gather annually to honor the memory of the guy who will never grow old because he died when he was only 21.

"My parents owned the neighborhood grocery store," explained Terry, "and Eddie's parents worked for them from time to time. That's how we kids met. Eddie, Dave Lindahl and I used to be like the three musketeers running around the neighborhood doing the kinds of things most kids do.

Terry Cole and Eddie Cochran
Sometime in the early 1940's.

We had a clubhouse down among the lilac bushes furnished with sling shots, rubber guns made of clothespins and pieces of inner tube, and a radio connected to an extension cord that ran from the house.

Eddie's older sister Gloria used to babysit. We caught fish by the channel, played cowboys and Indians, slid down the hill behind the jail on pieces of cardboard, and sneaked each other in to see cowboy movies at the Broadway or Rivoli on Saturday afternoons."

Eddie's musical education began at Ramsey School in Albert Lea, a town where folks gave just as much respect to a kid in the chorus, orchestra or band as they gave to the star quarterback. Albert Lea Public Schools' traveling voice teacher, Miss Hammock, visited each elementary school weekly to ensure that every kid got a chance to learn how to sing and gain exposure to music theory. Third graders learned to play flutophones. When Cap Emmons selected fifth graders to play trombones and clarinets, Eddie gave it a short try before rejecting those instruments in favor of the old Key guitar his brother left behind when he joined the Army. He also learned to play drums.

When he received a new guitar for Christmas, he brought it over to Terry Cole's house. By listening to an Eddy Arnold song, " Cattle Call," Eddie figured out how to play the chords and yodel the refrain. He bought a chord book, studied it, and started to become a musician. When he moved to California a couple of years later, at an age when most adolescents were thinking about what they wanted to do with the rest of their lives, Eddie already knew what he wanted to do. He became so good at doing something he loved that people started paying him to do it. He worked hard, and in a few years he became a rock and roll legend.

When I sat down to write this story, I looked on the internet for a discography of Eddie Cochran's recorded work, and I was further astounded when it took a half hour to scroll down the page and read about all the music credited to Eddie. In addition to writing and performing dozens of songs, Eddie played guitar, appeared in movies, and played or sang backup for scores of other artists from 1955 until 1960. He worked constantly from the time he was about 16 years old.

The Rock and Roll Hall of Fame inducted Eddie Cochran to membership in 1988, more than a quarter century after his untimely death. In retrospect, everyone realized that his contributions to music had inspired generations that followed. Whether he would have stood the test of time and remained a musical kingpin remains a matter of speculation. He died before he completed his first year as a full-fledged, legal adult.

At 21, Eddie Cochran was still having fun with his music. He had not yet fought the demons that plague some entertainers, nor had he been involved in any scandals. British fans were crazy about him. His records were topping British and American charts, and British crowds cheered and screamed at his concerts. The tour was extended a few more weeks, but he was becoming road-weary. Eddie called his mom and told her that he was homesick. He wanted to take a break and go home to see his family. He told her that nothing would stop him from coming home. En route to Heathrow airport, his car blew a tire and hit a tree. Eddie, who was thrown through the windshield, died later in a hospital.

Psychologists say that who we are and what we become is determined in large part by our early experiences. We learn to shun inferiority and adopt industry if we see that mastering skills will get us somewhere in this world. We are more likely to take risks and exercise creativity later in life if, during our formative years, possibilities are introduced as attainable goals. Education and encouragement at critical times in their lives enable artists to tweak what they know in order to create-- and thereby lead the rest of us into a place where we've never been before.

People who knew Eddie Cochran back when he lived on Charles Street remember him as a smart kid, a likable kid, a nice kid who liked to act things out, show off, and have fun.

Eddie (center) with Bill Melepsy and Merle McGuiniss

They remember the Cochran family as a close group. They still gather at block parties to remember Eddie and celebrate the fact that they may have helped provide just a little bit of the influence that pushed him beyond most people's scope. They chuckle about how poor they all were and how they had to invent their fun. They recall how their neighborhood was home to people of different ethnic backgrounds at a time when the rest of Albert Lea wasn't very diverse. They remember the huge crowd of kids who lived on Charles Street, and how their parents gave them freedom to explore their world without supervision. The only rule was that at the end of their busy day, they had to come home for dinner.

Truth is indeed more wonderful than fiction. A poor little kid from a big family in Albert Lea, Minnesota picks up a guitar and teaches himself to play. As amazing as it sounds, he rises to fame and influence in a new musical genre called rock and roll. He calls his mom to say he's homesick and wants to take a break from his hectic performance schedule. On his way home, he dies in an accident. His old friends still gather to remember him. Movie producers would probably reject this screenplay as unbelievable.

The Rock and Roll Hall of Fame in Cleveland has inducted two Minnesota solo artists. Most music fans around the world would be able to come up with the name of the other native son, Bob Dylan, but they might be surprised to learn that Eddie Cochran was the first Minnesota native whose work earned him a place in the Hall of Fame. Dylan moved to New York and launched his career after Eddie's death in 1960 and has enjoyed nearly a half century of successful work. His induction into the Hall of Fame came a year after the induction of Eddie Cochran.

In their summary of Eddie's life and career achievements, Hall of Fame copywriters said, " Eddie Cochran left a lasting mark on rock and roll as a pioneer who helped map out the territory with such definitive songs as "C'mon Everybody," "Something Else," "Twenty Flight Rock" and " Summertime Blues." But they also said he was born in Oklahoma.

It's time to set the record straight. A memorial erected near his boyhood home by his old friends and neighbors says it best.

" *Albert Lea remembers Eddie Cochran, who was born here in 1938, moved to California in 1952, and became one of rock 'n' roll's greatest pioneers. We will never forget him.* "

Albert Lea native Eddie Cochran was one of the first inductees into the Rock and Roll Hall of Fame and the first Minnesota native whose music earned him that distinction. For us pop culture aficionados, that's a piece of Minnesota history worth remembering.

The Late Great Eddie Cochran
Born in Albert Lea, Minnesota, 1938
Died near London, England, 1960

All photos courtesy of Terry Cole

Halo is the Shampoo that Glorifies Your Hair
by Joan Claire Graham

I wash my hair every day in the shower. This simple act takes only a couple of minutes and is so much a part of my daily routine that I don't even think about it. However, I vividly recall a time in my youth when hair washing was a major ordeal that required the better part of a day for setup, planning, execution and recovery.

Perhaps it was because we had no shower in our old Albert Lea house--not even one of those hand-held rubber spraying contraptions that fasten onto the tub spigot. My mother considered hair washing to be a major undertaking. Perhaps it was because she washed my hair so seldom that she never acquired any skills or professional knowhow. For whatever reason--in her appraisal of chores, hair washing and constructing the Brooklyn Bridge merited identical difficulty ratings.

My mother dusted her furniture every day, and she made me clean the silverware drawer and dust the mop boards every Saturday. She was an absolute clean freak regarding all things inanimate. The dishes were washed, dried, and put away three times a day, the floor was mopped two or three times a week, and the sheets and clothes were washed every Monday. But the hair that grew from my head and sopped up body oils and sweat from the inside and dust, sneeze germs, and mosquito spray from the outside, got cleaned far less frequently. This was partly due to the commonly held belief at that time that hair should not be washed often and partly because washing hair at our house was just such a big deal.

To help her cope with the huge task of washing my hair, my mother collected an arsenal of tools and techniques. The first tool I recall was a plastic halo that was supposed to keep shampoo out of a child's eyes. We used Halo brand shampoo, a frequently advertised product on popular radio shows. Halo jingle singers sang, "Halo everybody, Halo. Halo is the shampoo that glorifies your hair," and sometimes the shampoo company had special mail-in offers for products to help glorify your life even further. I think Mom ordered our plastic children's hair washing halo from the Halo shampoo company.

For some strange reason, children were thought to be incapable of just keeping their eyes closed or ducking their heads so that shampoo and rinse water went down the drain without getting into their eyes. I confess to having been incapable of keeping my eyes shut, primarily because I believed, during the ordeal of hair washing, that I had a slim chance of coming out of the experience alive. Opening my eyes was my first line of defense.

I remember using that plastic eye-protecting halo during my early years, but it certainly didn't work. One problem was that plastic products in those days were brittle and scratchy. Another problem was that one size definitely didn't fit all, so when I put it on, it felt like I had my head in a vise. The biggest problem, however, was that if I jammed my head through that brittle piece of plastic, the halo inevitably got in the way when Mom tried to wash my hair. How could it not get in her way? It was on my head, and she was trying to wash my head.

Picture a child standing tiptoe on a Montgomery Wards catalog atop a chair in front of the kitchen sink with a plastic halo on her head and her head aiming toward the sink. Mother tries to gingerly apply shampoo just on top of the head, to avoid the sides where the halo is attached. However, as Mom begins to lather up, the plastic becomes lubricated and the halo starts slipping all over the place. Then Mom, figuring that she may as well grit her teeth, bear down, and finish what she started out to do, takes the plunge, rips the halo off, and does what needs to be done.

Once my halo was gone, I was compelled to take a peek at what was happening to me, and when the shampoo inevitably drizzled into my curious eyes, I screamed in pain and twisted to get away. A struggling child triggered Mom's defense mechanisms, causing her to become even more tense and determined to finish the job, grab onto the child any way she could, and issue threats. This action produced panic, which produced more struggling and more threats. The shrieking and torquing and resulting splashing probably wore Mom out and led her to reconsider the bi-weekly time frame of hair washing frequency and stretch it to monthly-- or whenever everybody recovered.

One urban legend or old wives' myth that Mom strictly adhered to was the belief that at the end of each hair washing treatment, when all soap had at last been rinsed from squeaky clean hair, and the child was at last subdued, the hair washer needed to inflict one last act of torture. To close the pores, Mother believed, the hair washer had to dump a cup of absolutely cold water onto the head of the washee. A variation involved a tablespoon of vinegar added to the cold water. The shrieks from this final act were of a higher pitch than previous protest sounds and usually ended when a terry towel enveloped the clean little head.

When I outgrew the halo, mom simply made me hold a wash rag over my eyes, which never worked very well either. She didn't have any kind of spraying device, and she was so awkward when dumping cup after cup of rinse water over my head--first too hot--then to cold--that the scene inevitably dissolved into chaos and splashing that turned the kitchen floor into a pond.

Another hair washing tool Mother tried was a hard rubber scrubber. Perhaps because my dirty hair looked so bad, she figured a good deep scrubbing might keep my hair clean longer. Although the rubbery scrubbing teeth felt relatively soft to the touch, they felt like a crown of thorns on my wet scalp. Someone accidentally tossed that tool into the trash when someone else wasn't looking, so we spent much time pretending to try to find it, and Mom finally gave up looking and reverted to digging her fingernails into my scalp to try to dislodge deep grime and dirt.

One of Mom's friends suggested that she move me down from my tippy catalog and chair tower and lay me on the kitchen counter with my head hanging back into the sink. That way, all my hair would cascade into the sink, with all shampoo and water away from my eyes and following the laws of gravity--flowing down the drain. In theory this sounds reasonable, but in practice it was scary. To a child, the counter top is a very high altitude. Lying up there on the kitchen cupboard with my eyes covered by a wash rag and with my neck resting on the porcelain sink edge and my head dangling backwards toward the drain that I feared I might fall into was terrifying and painful. When my dad got home, he objected to seeing me like that on the kitchen counter--not because he thought I might be suffering, but because he thought it was unsanitary.

Mother complied with Dad's health directive, but she found an alternative to the cupboard --the ironing board. She propped the narrow end of her wobbly wooden ironing board up on the sink edge and laid me up there. I felt like Wendy Darling in *Peter Pan* walking the plank blind-folded as I clutched my little washrag over my eyes and crept up the iron-ing board toward the sink.   Wendy got to walk the plank on her feet, whereas I had to endure the additional challenge of lying down and scoot-ing backwards till my head fell backwards over the edge and dangled into the sink.   I was terrified on that narrow ironing board as it teetered on its two back legs.

Ignoring the fact that I was scared out of my mind, Mom felt she had finally figured out how to wash a child's hair, and long after I out-grew the ironing board, she repeated this procedure with my little sister Ann.   Ann would see the ironing board emerge from the closet and take off running like a bat out of hell. Mom enlisted my help in capturing Ann and hoisting her up and holding her onto the precariously perched ironing board. Throughout the hair washing ordeal, the usually serene little girl would twist and scream so loudly that neighbors once knocked on the door to ask if we were murdering her.   Despite the concern of neighbors, Mom continued washing Ann's hair like that until she became too big to lie on the ironing board.

After the frigid water had been applied and the shrieking had sub-sided, the shampoo experience was far from over.   Creme rinses, which effectively untangle hair, had not yet made their way to the shelves of Albert Lea retailers, so the next step after the Arctic rinse involved the detangling process. Mom extracted excess water by roughly rubbing a terry towel all over clean hair, which increased tenfold the mass of tangles that had been created by the washing process.

Mom bought combs at Woolworths in multi-packs. We didn't lose combs; we destroyed them when we pulled their teeth out with our tangles.   More shrieks, more threats, more tears. After detangling, we still had to endure the set-- and finally, the dry.

The natural look must have been frowned upon, because the next product Mom used after detangling was called Setting Lotion.   Setting Lotion, which had the consistency of snot, came in a wide-mouth bottle that you could dip a comb into, and the buyer could choose pink or clear Setting Lotion for the same low price of about 15 cents.

Taking one square inch of hair strands at a time, Mom dipped her comb into pink snot and combed the concoction through my hair. Then she placed her index finger on my scalp, wrapped the hair into a flat coiled circle, and fastened this neat little circle of hair to my scalp with an X made of two bobby pins. Rubber tipped bobby pins produced no pain, but the plain ones scratched and dug into the scalp, causing more outcries. If the person making the hair circles was not careful to tuck the end of the hair into the circle before applying bobby pins, the hair dried with what people used to derisively refer to as fishhook ends. Having fishhook ends was almost as bad as having worms or lice in those days.

Usually this entire hair ordeal took place on Saturday afternoon or evening, so I had to sleep on that nest of bobby pin X's in order to look spiffy for church. To make things even more uncomfortable, the bobby pinned hair was wet and covered with a hair net, and it took hours for the coils of hair to dry.

Nobody had hair dryers, but some folks tried creative alternatives. In summer, they sat out in the sunshine. In winter, some people tried to dry hair by sitting in front of an open, hot oven, and others had vacuum cleaners that blew air if you hooked the hose up to a different hole than the one that drew air in. We had one of those, but it didn't work very well. For one thing, the air was cold, and for another--the hose was dirty and it smelled like the machine was blowing dirt right back onto my hair that had just been so painstakingly washed.

When the hair finally dried, and bobby pins came off, and the resulting curls were brushed out, I had the glorified hair promised by Halo Shampoo ads. Of course, since we were Catholic, I had to wear a hat or scarf over my pretty curls when I went to church.

Unfortunately, after a couple of nights of getting slept on, my hair returned to its natural unglorified state, and as time wore on it became obvious that more glorification was needed--no matter what the cost in time and trauma. Thus began another cycle--the anticipation, the excuses to delay, (You were not supposed to wash hair if you had a cold, and I nearly always had one) the execution, (so to speak) and finally the recovery, followed by a couple of days of glorified hair.

Today things are so much simpler with showers, shampoos for-
mulated for every type hair, creme rinses and blow dryers. I can go from
unglorified to glorified in fifteen minutes with no halos, no rubber scrub-
bers, no tears, so soapy eyes, no ironing boards, no tangles, no broken
combs, no tantrums, and no sleepless nights with my head encased in
bobby pins and wet hair. How did I survive those torturous days and
nights that preceded a couple of days of Halo glorified hair? I don't even
want to think about it. This is one time when the good old days aren't
worth recreating.

Photo Courtesy of Colgate Palmolive: Janet Roys, Archivist

Television, the Eighth Wonder of the World
by Joan Claire Graham

Sister Benita asked my first grade class, "How many of you have television sets at your houses?" and seven of us put our hands in the air. It was a half century ago, the spring of 1953, and since Uncle Jack was scheduled to arrive at our house in Albert Lea with our new television that very day, I felt entitled to raise my hand and proud to be included among the privileged minority.

Two years earlier, my godparents in Henderson had been the first in the family to purchase a TV set. When we visited them to check out their marvelous investment, I became intrigued with this wonderful new entertainment that included midget wrestling, Minneapolis Laker basketball starring George Mikan, and "Arthur Godfrey's Talent Scouts." Shortly after my mother expressed interest in someday owning a television, her more impulsive sister Lex Klosterman ran right out and bought one, thereby beating Mom to the punch, as was her custom. But we were always welcome guests. I watched my first episodes of "I Love Lucy," Ed Sullivan's "Toast of the Town, " " I've Got a Secret," and " What's My Line?" at Klostermans' house across town.

My dad's brother Jack, who worked at Graybar Electric in Minneapolis, got good deals on television sets for family members. Since most of my aunts and uncles had taken advantage of this opportunity before my folks took the plunge, I assume there was sibling pride and rivalry involved in my parents' decision to buy a television set in 1953 without thinking about it for ten more years like they did with most other large purchases.

Even though Jack got us a good deal, a television in the early 50's was a major investment that had to be factored into the family budget. I recently bought a thirteen- inch color set with remote for $49, an amount I usually carry in my purse, but our twenty-inch console Hoffman with a maple cabinet cost more than $250 in 1953. At that time, our annual family income was approximately $5000, and $250 equaled a half year's mortgage payments. This purchase was not something to be taken lightly.

The price was not the only heavy aspect of the new television set. My dad and brother helped Uncle Jack unload the Hoffman from his huge two-tone Buick because it took two men and a boy to carry the thing. We eagerly anticipated the debut of new and endless possibilities of televised entertainment. The nearest major television stations were located in Minneapolis and St. Paul, a hundred miles north, but smaller towns were beginning to jump on the bandwagon and broadcast a few hours per day. Austin and Rochester had television stations, and later Mason City completed the three-network lineup.

Even though some signals originated less than twenty miles from Albert Lea, decent television reception was not a foregone conclusion. Viewers had to install metal antennas on their roofs. Some folks tried for better reception by purchasing an antenna that could be turned by remote control. Sometimes outside you would hear a mechanical hum, look up and see television antennas rotating on house tops. But even with the best antenna, the picture would start to roll and sound would turn to static if a storm was in the air, an airplane flew over, a neighbor turned on her Mixmaster, or, as urban legend had it, a Ford drove by the house. Viewers had to deal with reception interruptions all the time. We'd jump up, adjust the vertical or horizontal hold, turn the antenna remote, or give the set a smack--all of which worked sometimes-- but not always.

The set contained dozens of tubes--none of which lasted forever. The biggest was the picture tube, which cost almost as much to replace as an entire set. Television owners feared picture tube burnout nearly as much as they feared tornadoes, so they purchased picture tube insurance. When a smaller tube gave out, we'd call a man to come and replace it. Our repairman, Mr. Jewell, was almost the same size as the big doctor-type bag of tubes that he carried. After removing the back of the set, Mr. Jewell would test suspicious tubes until he found the dead one. A repair usually cost about ten dollars or less, depending on the tube or tubes that had to be replaced.

But repairs and maintenance were far from our minds the night we got our TV because we just wanted to see the darned thing work. By the time my dad and Uncle Jack hooked it up, it was too late and dark to install the antenna on the roof. But since Austin was only twenty miles away, we thought we might be able to pull in their signal anyway.

We turned on the set, but after a couple of minutes, the screen lit up with nothing but snow. What a disappointment! In a rare show of good sportsmanship, my brother grabbed the antenna wires and stood on the piano bench with arms outstretched. Suddenly the face and guitar of Johnny Western came into focus. Johnny, a teenage cowboy music singer, later caught the attention of Gene Autry and went on to film and recording success, but we saw him first singing "Red River Valley" in front of a bland curtain at Austin's KMMT television studio. Johnny Western was the first entertainer I saw on television in our Albert Lea living room.

In those days, large television stations that generated big city ad revenue produced quite a bit of local programming and signed on the air early to broadcast Dave Garroway and J. Fred Muggs on "The Today Show," but local stations didn't sign on until afternoon or early evening, and they usually signed off after the late news. Before signing on for the day, stations sent out a test pattern signal with recorded musical background. The geometric design of the pattern led a person to believe there was something scientific going on, but I think this was a ruse.

Local stations produced news, kids' shows like " Bart's Clubhouse," talent shows featuring free, live, home-grown tap dancers and piano players, school chorus concerts, and interviews with local civic and business leaders. In the evening they broadcast network programs.

We could usually pull in reception from the more powerful Twin Cities stations when local stations were signed off for the day. Minnesota sports events, including St. Paul Saints baseball, Minneapolis Lakers, University of Minnesota sports, pro wrestling, and the ever-popular state basketball tournament provided quality competition to network programming, and KSTP and WCCO broadcast state and national news.

Static news formats featured anchors sitting at desks reading copy, with very few visuals except for the anchor's name on the front of the desk and a station logo stuck to the back wall. With remote broadcast technology, today's trial story is likely to be delivered live by a reporter standing in front of a courthouse, but in those days we only saw video of spectacular stories like the St. Olaf's Church fire in downtown Minneapolis. That film was not live because it had to be processed before air time.

The folks at WCCO spruced up their static news broadcasts with a theatrical trick called the Shell Weather Tower. Music played as a long shot showed a tower with a platform on top, where a man stood with his back turned. The camera panned up the ladder as a voice intoned, "High atop the Shell Weather Tower........" And as the camera reached the platform and the back of the Shell weatherman writing on his map, there was a quick cut to show the back of Bud Kraehling, dressed in his Shell uniform and cap and standing in a little shack up there on the tower platform.

Bud noticed the arrival of his audience, turned around, looked out into the night air, and remarked how cold or hot it was or how many stars or city lights he could see from his perch on top of that tower. We believed that from his vantage point Bud could see those Canadian cold fronts rolling in or warn us of approaching tornadoes. Tourists spent hours driving around Minneapolis looking for the Shell Weather Tower, but in reality the tower and ladder were only an artist's rendering, and the shack where Bud hung out was a studio set. Stagehands sometimes threw snow or rain on Bud to assuage skeptics, and they sure had me fooled. I believed the Shell Weather Tower was real until I recently learned otherwise. I don't know where I thought the camera man was standing--clinging to the top rung of the ladder perhaps with his two hundred pound nonportable camera strapped to his shoulder?

Photo courtesy of Bud Kraehling and the Pavek Museum of Broadcasting

Television quickly became part of our lives.   Recognizing the entertainment and babysitting potential of children's programming, national programmers quickly expanded production to include daytime kids' shows like Pinky Lee and Howdy Doody.   Broadcast back to back, these shows had completely different formats.   Pinky Lee, a former vaudevillian, performed songs and dances and had adult contestants compete in games for prizes like irons and electric frying pans.   The game I most vividly remember involved three women wearing boxing gloves racing the clock while trying to install pillow cases.   I still think about that game whenever I change my pillowcases.   Pinky Lee featured Molly Bee, a cute teen country singer with a long pony tail and miles of crinolines under her circle skirts. We all thought she was terrific.

Buffalo Bob Smith and his marionette pals Howdy Doody, Dilly Dally, Summerfallwinterspring, Flubadub and Mr. Bluster led the kids in the peanut gallery in a rousing chorus of " It's Howdy Doody Time," and Clarabell the clown communicated by honking a bicycle horn.   Skits involved seltzer bottles, and marionette shows portrayed the lives and concerns of Howdy and the gang.

The first interactive Saturday morning children's show featured a cartoon character named Winky Dink.   Viewers sent for a Winky Dink kit, consisting of a crayon and a sheet of green see-through plastic that stuck to the TV screen. Following directions given by host Jack Barry, kids drew pictures on the screen that gave clues and tools to help Winky Dink get out of trouble.

Networks expanded their daytime programs to entertain housewives. Soap operas, " Queen for a Day," "Art Linkletter's House Party" most of which were carry-overs from radio, joined daytime program lineups. Daytime variety shows like "The Garry Moore Show," "The Jack Paar Show," and "The Tennessee Ernie Ford Show," and game and quiz shows cropped up. Later daytime additions included Dick Clark's "American Bandstand" and "Who Do You Trust?" starring young Johnny Carson.

When men came home from work, they could settle in to their easy chairs after supper and watch boxing matches on the " Gillette Cavalcade of Sports" or westerns like " Gunsmoke." Families learned history lessons when Walter Cronkite interviewed Abraham Lincoln and Salem witch trial participants on "You Are There." We laughed at Milton Berle, Jack Benny, Sid Caesar, Ernie Kovacs, Red Skelton and Jackie Gleason, and we held our collective breath and bit our nails waiting for Charles Van Doren, Dr. Joyce Brothers and Willy Shoemaker to come up with the right answers on "Twenty-one" and " The $64,000 Question."

We helped contestants " Name That Tune," and laughed when Groucho Marx traded witticisms with folks on " You Bet Your Life." "The Voice of Firestone" and Leonard Bernstein's Sunday concerts brought classical and semiclassical music into our homes, and "Your Hit Parade" and "The Lawrence Welk Show" performed their own renditions of the pops. Bishop Fulton J. Sheen preached, Nat King Cole sang, and Mr. Wizard demonstrated science lessons.

Ed Sullivan brought Broadway into our living rooms, and Steve Allen introduced Elvis Presley. "Hallmark Hall of Fame," "Climax," and "Playhouse 90" produced quality dramatic shows featuring young actors like Paul Newman. Local stations showed old movies, and the "Tonight Show" entertained insomniacs. There was something for everyone. Each station played the National Anthem before signing off for the night, as if to remind viewers that television had changed American lifestyles.

Critics accused television of ruining our imaginations. They said we would lose our ability and inclination to read and conduct conversations. Etiquette experts debated whether or not television should be turned off or left on when company dropped in. TV dinners and TV trays were invented. Educators warned about the effect of too much television viewing. Movie theatres lost money, and doctors warned us to sit at least six feet back so we wouldn't strain our eyes.

Twenty-five years after my family received our first television set, I took a survey among the students in my junior high speech class in Columbia Heights. Only one girl confessed to having no television set in her home, and when we added all the sets in all the homes and divided the total by the number of kids in the class, the average number of television sets was four per household. With today's cheaper solid state technology, I would guess that number has increased significantly, but viewer consensus about what constitutes a show worth watching has dispersed in all directions.

When "I Love Lucy" premiered in 1952, nearly 70% of potential viewers tuned in. Families sat around and watched hugely popular shows together, and everyone conducted conversations the next day about the common experience they had all shared from their respective living rooms. Nothing on television today attracts that kind of audience, and the hundreds of cable offerings, combined with several sets in most households produce a high likelihood that family members will scatter to their respective rooms to watch whatever they like.

While teenage daughter watches MTV in the family room, Mom watches a drama in the living room, Junior watches ESPN in his bedroom and Dad watches the History Channel in the den. Grandma calls about something she saw on The Cooking Network, and we tell her we'll have to watch it sometime if we can find it on our local cable channel guide.

I don't think anybody fifty years ago could have predicted the extent to which television would become part of our lives. We watched Queen Elizabeth's coronation and saw President Eisenhower take the oath of office in the 50's. We stayed glued to our sets during President Kennedy's funeral in the 60's. We saw graphic coverage of the Vietnam war in the 70's, and in the 90's we watched reporters dive for cover as Scud missiles threatened their safety live and in color on CNN during the Gulf War. We saw the Eifle Tower ablaze with pyrotechnics to celebrate hope and promise for a new millennium.

One late summer morning, as I sipped coffee and prepared to begin work on *Minnesota Memories 2*, "Today" host Matt Lauer announced that a plane had hit the World Trade Center. In the following days, I watched until I could not bear to watch any longer. And new viewer awareness followed as world reaction unfolded.

In the fifty years since Sister Benita asked our class that memorable question, television and life have changed tremendously. Television's popularity and availability have skyrocketed, the sophistication and flexibility of broadcasting have improved beyond our wildest imaginations, and the amount of programming has increased a hundred fold. The communication age swept us up and showed us things we never thought we'd see, and our friends under the age of 50 can not remember a time when television was not part of life.

Sal
by Joan Claire Graham

Southern Minnesota summers seemed to last forever when I was a kid in the 50's. The jubilation at the end of each school year and the excitement and relief of seeing written proof on the back of my final report card that I would, in fact, be promoted to the next grade soon gave way to the boredom of those long, hot, humid, mosquito-infested days.

All the Protestant kids in town were required to attend Vacation Bible School for the first two weeks each summer, but I was one of Albert Lea's tiny minority who attended Catholic school. Since our entire curriculum was religious, we did not have to attend Vacation Bible School. Therefore, unless we were lucky enough to live near one of the other Catholic kids, we were stuck for those first two weeks each summer with nobody to hang out with. Going to visit my grandmother Sal in Mankato seemed like a great solution to this problem.

We always called her Sal, never Grandma or any of those other names most kids called their elders. Her given name was Clara Lucia Troska, and she professed to like that name and was thrilled that my middle name was Claire. However, in her infancy her brothers and sisters--all eleven of them--had dubbed her Sally, and that was the name everybody in the family used until they shortened it to Sal. This strange custom of calling a person by a name other than his or her given name was rampant in her hometown of Minnesota Lake, near Mankato.

Although my grandmother lived only fifty miles away, this distance was considered enough of a trek to make any visit seem special, so a two-week stay at her house felt like a major getaway. There were no kids my age who lived in her neighborhood, so any time I spent in Mankato was time spent with Sal, which was fine with both of us.

My grandmother, who was in her 70's, had been a widow for several years before I was born. She was extremely independent despite the fact that she never owned a car and never, since before her marriage in 1907, held a job. After the death of her husband, she got together with her sister and bought a big house in Mankato. When her sister died, and with her children raised, Sal had the house to herself. With thrift and ingenuity, she managed quite comfortably for over a quarter century.

Although she received a small pension from her late husband's work and a yearly check from the farmer who leased her homestead in North Dakota, she financed most of her daily life by renting out two big upstairs bedrooms to girls attending the Mankato Business School. The slightly bigger room went for twenty dollars a month; the smaller one rented for three dollars less. Two girls usually lived in each room.

The business college girls attended a one-year program, so there were always new roomers to contend with. They brought youth and laughter into the house and prevented the place from becoming too stuffy. I wasn't supposed to go upstairs and bother them, but I confess to snooping through their eyelash curlers and lipsticks when they were away. My grandmother's activities fit very nicely into the five rooms and full-sized basement downstairs.

I spent two weeks in early June each year with Sal in her big house on Washington in Mankato, down in the valley in the old part of town. Mankato's days and nights were even hotter than those in my hometown, but the place had its charm. Across the street was a school playground with big swings, a slide and a merry-go-round. On the corner stood Joseph's, a little family-owned grocery store that sold everything, including penny candy. Despite our lack of transportation, Sal and I managed to get around to any place we wanted to go.

In spite of her age, Sal walked briskly, and we would often walk to one of the nearby movie theaters. Unlike my parents, Sal never bothered to take notice of whether the Legion of Decency had rated a film A1, A2 or B. She probably figured she was beyond corruption, which was true, and she acted like there was no difference in age between us.

We walked downtown, where three dime stores stood in a row, and we bought yard goods at Bretts Department Store. One time she took me square dancing at the armory, and of course we often walked up the hill to attend mass at St. Peter and Paul Church. She took me along when she walked to the old folks home, where she tried to teach ladies how to crochet. She called them, " old ladies," even though some were younger than she was. I don't think Sal was too crazy about kids, so I tried not to act like one in any way that would annoy her. She didn't talk down to me or make any rules about bedtime. We just hung out together.

Sal had a number of irons in the fire, not the least of which was her rich social life. Because of her location near downtown Mankato, Minnesota Lake cousins stopped in whenever they visited the bigger town to shop. Sal always had a story to tell, was happy to listen to their stories, and she inevitably offered each visitor a cookie and a cup of tea, served on her best china.

In addition to visiting relatives, Sal also belonged to a number of church groups and a group of ladies who played cards. She sewed all her own clothes, tatted lace, made soap from lye and meat fat saved for her by the corner grocer, canned tomatoes and other vegetables, made pies and bread, knitted and crocheted mittens and scarves, wrote letters, braided rugs made from scraps cut from our castoff clothes, made crazy quilts and painted beautiful pictures. Her easel was always set up in the dining room, and all her descendants have at least one of her paintings hanging in their homes.

Sal at her easel when she was in her 80's.

One evening, as I listened to the radio and she arranged her painting supplies, a bat swooped through the living room. I bolted out the door and ran down to Broad Street as if my pants were ablaze because I have a phobia of mammals with wings, but Sal, nonplused, got out her broom and shooed the bat outside. Afterwards she derided me for being such a coward, and I thought her assessment of my character was accurate.

My mother wanted me to learn bread baking from Sal, but whenever I asked her to show me how, she'd reply, "H'aint nothin' to it. A handful of this, a pinch of that." Her hands flew as she demonstrated, but she had no recipes written on paper. When I'd ask her to teach me how to sew, she'd haul out her machine, scissors, and a scrap of cloth and make me a dress for my Tiny Tears doll. She was a doer, not a teacher.

She was never idle. If she wasn't engaged in housework or one of her arts or crafts, her hands would start to drum impatiently on the arm of the chair. While she drummed, the wheels of her imagination turned. Eventually she would find something to make or some work to do. She stubbornly mispronounced a few words, a habit that I tried to correct. But no matter how many times I tried to stop her, she still said, "Shears and Roebuck," and a few other funny words.

She scorned "adamatic" washing machines and insisted on doing all laundry for herself and her roomers with an old hand-wringer machine. She hung her wash outside each Monday morning, exchanging conversation with neighbors engaged in the same task. If it rained, she'd hang the wet clothes in the basement. Whenever she bought new sheets, she would rip out the large top hem and make it the same size as the bottom hem. That way, she could put the sheets on the beds without having to figure out which end was which, but more importantly she could rotate   and wear them out more evenly. She assured me that if I had lived during the Depression, this time- consuming practice would make sense.

She did not own a television set until her grown kids pooled their money and bought her one in 1963. But even after she got TV, she preferred radio news, music, and political discussions. She liked her radio, she said, because she could listen while she did all those other things. Television, she complained, required you to take your eyes off your work.

If she took her eyes off her work, she preferred reading. In addition to the *Mankato Free Press,* she subscribed to the *Readers Digest,* the *Catholic Digest,* and some mission magazines. Her friends gave her their old copies of *Life, Look,* and *Saturday Evening Post. Readers Digest* sent her their collections of condensed novels, and she owned quite a few literary classics.

Until she was in her mid-80's, she remained agile and independent. One time she was riding in a VW Beetle driven by a roomer who had convinced her to check out a downtown antique store. As they crossed an intersection, a car going the other way collided with the Beetle, which was so airtight that the impact caused the passenger door to fly open and my grandmother to fly out. As she landed on the sidewalk, her main concern was that her dress had flown up to expose her underwear. A policeman convinced her, amidst protest, to accept an ambulance ride to the hospital because he couldn't imagine that she wasn't hurt after being airborne and landing on cement. Despite her opposition to the plan, she needed to be checked out by doctors.

When she got into the ambulance, the driver asked whether she preferred to go to the Catholic or the Lutheran hospital. Since the Lutheran hospital was only a block from her house, she figured she could walk home from there after proving that she was no worse for the wear.

The police report that went out over KTOE radio frightened her friends. When they heard that she had been taken to the Lutheran hospital, they figured she must be near death because if she had been conscious, she would have never allowed herself to be treated by Lutherans. When she heard her story being broadcast on the radio, she objected to the newscaster's reference to her as, " Clara Eaton, an elderly Mankato woman." After walking home from the hospital, she settled up with the insurance adjustor for the ambulance ride, the emergency room exam, and $20, and thought she had made a killing. The only things damaged had been her dignity and a pair of nylons, and they only cost a dollar.

But her high spiritedness and ability to look upon life as a big adventure did not last forever. Eventually age and health problems forced her to give up her independence, and with her independence gone, her positive disposition deteriorated. My sister and cousins, who are ten years younger than I, do not remember her the same way I do. They missed out on Mankato summers and never knew the whirling dervish of a grandma who lives in my memory.

Although I love to recall all the neat things I did with Sal, the best part about our time together occurred in late evenings when she would start to tell stories about the old days. She was a night owl. By that time of day, the house would be so quiet that the sound of her voice would take on a whole new character, and she would be just reflective enough and comfortable enough after all her daily exertion to bring up stories of her childhood and young adulthood.

She told me about her life on the farm and about a school chum who flirted with a boy named Peter.   She told me about speaking Polish at home until she grew old enough to go to school. She told me about her mother's death, and about the death of her little brother. She told about her life as a young milliner in Minnesota Lake. And best of all, she told the epic tale of herself and three girl cousins who boarded a train in Minneapolis, and got off at a place called Bowbells, North Dakota, where they lived for two years and staked homestead claims in 1905. Nobody believed that young girls could accomplish such a feat, but they did.

Although she encouraged me to record her stories for posterity, she went to her grave at age 91 knowing that I had failed to do so.   She tried to prime the pump by furnishing me with notes she took, and I tried to turn those notes into stories several times, but I always gave up because I just couldn't manage to stay motivated.

Knowing how memory can play tricks as we grow older, and realizing that I may be one of the few people left who can write her stories from first hand accounts, I finally finished the task. But after I recorded some of Sal's stories, I felt I had to write something about the woman herself.   So with that softened impressionistic focus that the passage of time provides, I finally wrote what I remember of this remarkable woman and her friendship with me during the springtime of my life and the autumn of hers, framed forever in my memory by those long, hot summer days we shared in Mankato so many years ago.

20th Century Icons --Where Are They Now?
by Joan Claire Graham

My sister was helping the teacher at her son's elementary school a couple of years ago. The kids had been reading a short story that contained the following sentence: "After the movie, the boys came home and played some records." My sister was surprised that none of the kids knew what that meant.

When she told me about this incident, I started to think about all the icons of 20th Century pop culture that are no longer recognized by children, and I started to make a list, starting with phonographs and records.

Of all things on my list, the loss of phonographs and records bothers me the most. My mother won two phonographs in the 1940's, so I started playing records when I was a tiny child. Our first phonograph, a portable, weighed about twenty pounds and had a brown leatherette case with a sturdy handle so adults could carry it from room to room. This little machine was a big step towards miniaturization after the big consoles and windup victrolas that preceded it. When 45's replaced the heavier and more breakable 78 r.p.m. records, Mom won another drawing and we got a high fidelity sound when we plugged our little 45 changer into a sound jack on the back of our television. When 33 r.p.m. LP's gained popularity, we invested in stereo components and bought albums, not only for the music, but also for their cover art and notes.

Records, which gained popularity in the early 1900's, went through several upgrades but remained popular until they were edged out by smaller and lighter tapes and CD's in the 80's and 90's. It is now difficult or impossible to buy new records, and kids don't even know what the phrase, "play some records" means.

The mechanical revolution extended into other gadgets that became popular in the 20th century. Machines like televisions, radios and telephones operated with rotating dials. Radio and television announcers said, "Don't touch that dial," when they wanted listeners to stay tuned, and *Dial M for Murder* was a popular play and Hitchcock movie. With today's touch button technology, many young people have never dialed a phone.   Many have never heard a phone actually ring.   The old phones rang like bells; they didn't beep, squeal or play " Yankee Doodle Dandy."

Another item that has gone the way of the dinosaur is the type-writer.   Although the typewriter was invented much earlier, there wasn't much mass production or standardization of typewriters and keyboards until the early 1900's.   Young adults, mostly women, went off to be trained as typists, a respectable profession.   Businesses and the armed services relied on typewriters and carbon paper for reports and correspondence. Office supply stores sold a wide selection of typing ribbons and typing erasers that consisted of a coarse eraser and a crumb brush.   White-out and correcting tape were welcome innovations in the 1960's.

High school students crowded into typing classes, where teachers encouraged touch typing by installing charts at eye level and painting out the letters to make sure students didn't peek at the keys. They played music to encourage even, regular key strokes and led students through drills, ("Semi, semi, semi, a, a, a, l, l, l, s, s, s") designed to help the typist inter-nalize the keyboard arrangement.   Typing books showed how to format different kinds of papers and letters, set tabs, and correct errors.   Teachers conducted and evaluated weekly speed tests and every typing student knew exactly how many words per minute he or she could type.

A typist had to take her right hand off the keyboard every time she got to the end of a line of type in order to push the carriage return.   A bell warned that only a few more strokes were possible before the carriage refused to move.   In a second, the typist had to decide whether to push the carriage return, finish the word she was typing, or hyphenate.   If she chose to hyphenate, she had to do it at the grammatically appropriate place. If she chose to finish the word and the word contained too many strokes, she risked making a mistake that would take time to fix.

Portable typewriters became popular gifts for college bound high school graduates.   Only one font for each brand of typewriter was avail-able, but customers could choose it in either pica or elite size.   Two-color ribbons shifted to red or black ink, but the black always wore out before the red and poor college students hated to shell out money for a new one.

A secretary who could cut a clean stencil or ditto was a valued employee because those inventions made it possible to cheaply mass produce written communication. To cut a really good stencil, a typist needed a sturdy upright. Stencil cutters got a cleaner cut if they typed blindly with no ribbon, and correcting mistakes was tricky. They had to remove or peel back the stencil from its backing, read the carbon copy on the back of the stencil, paint a liquid over the mistake on the stencil, put the stencil carefully back into the machine, try to line everything up exactly as before, and strike over the error. It was difficult to get this right.

Ditto masters were a little less cumbersome than stencils, but they yielded fewer clean copies. To correct a mistake on a ditto master, the typist had to turn the master over and scratch the mistake off the paper with a little stylus that looked like a small matte knife. School kids could always tell when the teacher gave them copies fresh from the ditto or stencil machine because they were cold and they smelled like alcohol.

Professional typewriter servicing and cleaning cost a pretty penny, but it was worth the expense because after a while the lead slugs attached to the hammers that hit the ribbon that hit the paper became gummed up with old carbon, causing the open spaces on letters to cloud up.

The sound of clattering typewriter keys resounded in the halls of high schools and colleges and in libraries and college dorms. Newsrooms were a cacophony of carriage returns, bells, clattering keys and the final sound of paper being ripped from the carriage. Concert audiences cheered LeRoy Anderson's song, "The Typewriter" which incorporated all the sounds and rhythms of typing. Orchestras like the Boston Pops still play that song, but audiences listen with the same nostalgia associated with Anderson's other hit, " Sleigh Ride." The typewriter was definitely an icon of the 20th Century, but few people still use them.

Electric typewriters eased the strain of pushing down keys on manual models, and typewriter innovations in the 70's and 80's brought us more sophisticated machines. Towards the end of the century, however, those of us who had something to write became enticed by a new typing machine that allowed us to correct our mistakes more easily, do our work more quietly, press down keys with less strain on our hands and wrists, check our spelling before going to press, and create professional looking publications without messy ditto masters and stencils. Computers have replaced most typewriters, but some purists still prefer to use an Underwood upright.

The revolution in writing was not limited to machines. Fountain pens were the staple tool for handwriting for the greater part of the 20th Century. Fountain pens evolved from those that had to be dipped in ink every few seconds to those with snorkels and rubber bladders for loading and storing ink. School desks were designed with inkwells, and students practiced their Palmer method handwriting with fountain pens filled with washable or permanent ink that cost about a quarter. Black, blue-black and blue were acceptable colors. Periwinkle, green, and red ink, although more attractive at the store, were forbidden in school.

In 1971, Melanie sang, " I've got a brand new pair of roller skates; you've got a brand new key." Although listeners put Freudian interpretations to the song's meaning, everybody knew about roller skates and keys. The roller skates I received for Christmas in 1950 were similar to the ones my mom got before World War I except that mine had ball bearings in the steel wheels.

Roller skates could be sized by taking a key, which had a little hex wrench on one end, and loosening the nut that allowed the two parts of the skate bed to move back and forth. Roller skates could be tightened to grip the toe area of any shoe with a four-sided key wrench on the other end of the key. A leather or nylon strap tightened around the ankle. Skaters, who wore keys on strings or lanyards around their necks, had to master athletic and mechanical skills. You could hear a kid coming with his steel wheels rolling on concrete. It was generally understood that one pair of roller skates would be enough for any child.

Shoe skates with wooden wheels were expensive and were generally for indoor use, and most roller rink skaters rented skates. Roller Rats, the kids who skated every week, bought their own skates and stored them in neat metal cases. Towns as small as Witoka (population about 100) had roller rinks, and indoor roller skating was a popular activity. Some rinks employed organists and others played records while skaters courted and cavorted around the rink. Afternoons were for little kids and families, but Saturday and Friday nights were best for dates.

A Minnesota hockey player, Scott Olson, pioneered the early in-line skate that evolved into Rollerblades. Today's skates have polyurethane wheels that are permanently fastened to boots that kids outgrow, and today's skate rolls along smoothly and quietly. Keys are not needed. I have one that I wear on a chain around my neck when I talk at historical societies. People start conversations by asking, " Is that a skate key?"

For many decades, bottle openers were essential kitchen items. Hardware stores gave away bottle openers decorated with store logos. People mounted sturdy openers on cupboards and door frames. When beer and pop drinkers switched to canned beverages, their tops had to be punctured with a triangular opener. A tool euphemistically known as the church key had a bottle opener on one end and a can opener on the other. Pop machines at public places had an attached opener with a box that collected bottle caps. Kids used to play with and collect bottle caps. One thing we did was remove the cork lining of the cap all in one piece. We put the flat piece of cork on the inside of a shirt and the bottle top on the outside. We pushed the cork disk into the cap through the fabric to fasten the cap to the fabric for decoration. We had to remember to take off the decorations before the shirt went through the wash, because the bottle cap would leave a rust stain if it got wet, causing mom to have a fit.

Throughout most of the 20th century, females over the age of 3 demonstrated their refinement and decency by appearing in church and at other public gatherings with that wardrobe necessity we no longer see often--white gloves. Department stores stocked entire glass showcases with various designs and sizes of white gloves, and no respectable female appeared in public without them. My mother kept her white gloves in a special box in her dresser, and when she washed them, she inserted forms that prevented the gloves from shrinking. When I attended Winona State in the 60's, the dress code for St. Teresa's stated that girls had to wear white gloves when they went downtown. I don't know when women stopped wearing white gloves--probably about the same time they stopped wearing other items of clothing that we used to think were important.

Sears Roebuck and Montgomery Wards catalogs used to feature pages and pages of girdles, a garment that evolved from corsets that had kept women uncomfortable and semi-immobile for centuries. Women wore girdles for most of the 20th Century. Some girdles wrapped around the body from under the bust to beneath the butt. Some maintained rigidity with stays made of bone or plastic, and some included a bra. Some laced up, others zipped or fastened with hooks and eyes. All were torturous. No decent woman appeared in public without cinching herself in. I don't know where all the fat went when women were bound in like that, but I remember a lot of discomfort from pinching and from gas. When my mother and her friends got together to play bridge, they usually spent quite a bit of time tugging on and complaining about their girdles.

The girdles I wore in my youth, when I never weighed more than 110 pounds, were panty girdles with garters for holding up stockings. I can remember climbing out of my girdle and stockings at the end of the day and dealing with painful craters caused by those awful little rubber garter knobs digging into my thighs all day.

No decent woman, even a thin one, would go out without her girdle. It was wrong to have curves or a body that looked like it might contain human cells. Before World War II, girdles were made of rubber. During the war, when rubber was rationed, women with torn girdles took them to gas stations to have them patched like inner tubes.

Speaking of inner tubes, that's another icon that's disappeared. Today's steel belted radial tires are safer, but kids no longer have those great old inner tubes we used for winter hill sliding and summer water floats.

The same stores that sold girdles and white gloves sold hats. Take a look at any picture of a first lady from Alice Roosevelt until Betty Ford, and there's a good chance she's wearing a hat. We all wore hats when we went to church, went shopping, or went out for an evening. Buying a hat for the season was a ritual and a pleasure.

Men wore hats too, but they weren't as colorful, and men didn't need a new one every spring and fall. Men's hats came in an assortment of sizes with numbers and fractions. An old joke about picking a baby's name out of a hat had the kid christened Six and Three Eighths. Men wore hats when they went out, and church pews were equipped with clamps that held hats out of harm's way so that they wouldn't be accidentally sat on and squashed. Men took good care of their hats and even had them cleaned and blocked from time to time. While we're talking about fashion, let's mention overshoes and rubbers. Minnesotans wore these over their shoes so that their shoes would stay dry and last longer. They weren't always attractive, but they worked.

And remember hankies? Inside a birthday card would be tucked a pretty hanky. Some were embroidered; some had lace trim. Girls learned to iron by practicing on hankies. Miss Thompson, my kindergarten teacher at North Side Elementary School in Albert Lea, instructed us to pin a hanky to our dress or shirt. We used those hankies to blow our noses. No wonder nobody ever wanted to hug us!

Okay, I think I'm starting to sound a little too much like Andy Rooney. The items described were used for more than half the 20th Century and are not always recognized by today's kids. There must be more items that fit this description. How about if we make this story interactive? Readers who have items to add are invited to send their ideas for publication in *Minnesota Memories 4*.

How many items from this story can you see in this photo? The roller skates on my feet and girdle beneath my clothes don't count because they can't be seen.

Rufus and Sadie
by Joan Claire Graham

I knew exactly what I wanted to help transform my first house into a home--a black and white female kitten that would grow to be the perfect cat. I checked the Minneapolis Tribune classified ads and called a rescue organization that gave me phone numbers of several members who had rescued black and white female kittens that were up for adoption.

The first four numbers I dialed proved fruitless, but I tried one final number. A woman who answered said that she did indeed have a sweet little long-haired female kitten. A little boy in south Minneapolis had found it shivering in the rain and, knowing she took in strays, brought it to her. She described it as one of the nicest cats she'd ever rescued.

I hit light traffic and easily found her house within the hour. As she opened her door, I observed a highly illegal number of feline eyes looking hopefully toward me. She scooped up one little cat, suggested I get to know it out on her stoop, and closed the door to the multitude of the unchosen.

I always imagine I have a photograph of myself sitting on that step holding a long haired black and white kitten that purred and clung to me, but of course no such photo ever existed. It took less than a minute to decide that this was the cat for me. I named her Elizabeth in honor of another black and white cat that had met an untimely death, and I vowed to do better with this one.

On my way home to Robbinsdale, I stopped and bought a box of Tender Vittles. When I put it on the car seat, the previously docile little kitten tore the box and ripped open an envelope of food. She appeared to be starving, her appetite curiously disproportionate to her size.

The rescue organization's policy was that I paid them, and they gave me a voucher for a discount on a vet exam, vaccinations and eventual spaying. For the first week or two, I was the vet's best customer because Elizabeth's ears were clogged with mites, her belly was full of worms, and her fur was infested with fleas. I was afraid she might lose her sweet disposition, but she patiently endured, with only momentary lapses of purring, even temper, and affection, having her various body parts purged of vermin.

Elizabeth continued to eat prodigious amounts, grow, acquire a glorious long coat, and thrive. She was an affectionate lap cat who seemed unflappable. She had obviously been someone's pet before she was found starving and wandering in the rain. Everyone remarked how dainty and feminine she was, how clean and friendly.

I returned to my teaching job in September and felt bad about leaving Elizabeth alone all day, so in October I stopped at the Humane Society in Golden Valley and adopted Sadie, a tiny brown tortoise tabby short hair. When I walked into the house with the new kitten, Elizabeth experienced a personality transformation. She bared her fangs, arched her back, fluffed her tail, laid back her ears, and set up a caterwaul that seemed like it could not possibly be coming from this feminine and gentle little creature. I was astounded as she hissed and growled, and poor little Sadie was terrified.

I was afraid Elizabeth would kill the new kitten, so I kept the two separated for the first couple of weeks. When Sadie failed to grow and thrive, I decided to socialize the two cats. Sadie responded with a burst of growth and energy, and Elizabeth quickly warmed up to her. Before long, they curled up together for naps and washed the tops of each other's heads.

According to my schedule of anticipated veterinary procedures, Elizabeth had finished her series of vaccinations and parasite treatments, and was due to be spayed. I made the appointment, feeling guilty about subjecting this sweet animal to pain and separation just when she was starting to relax and enjoy herself with Sadie. On the day before the scheduled procedure, as she was rolling around on the carpet, stretching, and enjoying life--oblivious to her upcoming surgical ordeal, I noticed something that had never caught my eye before. As she lay there on her back with her legs spread wantonly, I noticed that Elizabeth had a penis.

I changed Elizabeth's name to Rufus, and he immediately became less dainty and more studly. But his studliness was short lived because I called the vet, and after we had a good laugh, we changed the upcoming operation to a neutering--which was by far cheaper and less invasive. Neither of us could figure out how we had missed the obvious during all those office visits.

As winter wore on, Rufus and Sadie strengthened their bond and picked up a few bad habits, the worst of which was their tendency to groom their claws on furniture. Since I don't believe in declawing or letting cats go outside, I opted for providing legal indoor surfaces for them to scratch. My husband built a spring-loaded, multi-shelved, carpet covered, floor-to-ceiling pole in the corner of the dining room. The cats played, slept, and climbed on the pole, and even developed a few tricks.

We were entertaining dinner guests one evening when all of a sudden everyone stopped talking and stared up at the curtain rod. Sadie had launched herself from a cat pole shelf onto the curtain rod over the window opposite the dining room table and was carefully tightrope walking over to the other side. But when she reached the end of the rod, she encountered a problem. She was eight feet up--too high to jump down to the floor, and she couldn't turn around and go back. If she turned toward the wall, she hit her head, and if she turned toward the room, she hit her butt on the wall. She tried it both ways a dozen times. With six pairs of eyes watching, and six people laughing, she had a go at backing across the curtain rod until I took mercy and rescued her. I thought she was embarrassed, but she repeated that trick whenever we had company. What a floor show--no cover charge, no minimum.

Another trick Rufus and Sadie perfected was fetching things. When the house was dark and the people were snoring, they'd roam around the house finding things to bring us in our beds. For a while they brought us potatoes from the basement--two flights up. I rolled over one night onto a sprouted potato and thought it was a critter. Another time I found Rufus curled up with a potato in the bathroom sink. When they tired of potatoes they started bringing up everything that was sitting on the kitchen counter.

I'd hear a rattle and open my eyes to see a cat with a bag of chips. One time they brought a bag of brownies upstairs and left it by the side of the bed. We started putting bakery goods in kitchen drawers after that.

Their fetching behavior wasn't always annoying. We had bats in the attic, and sometimes one would drop through a wall and swoop through the house. Rufus and Sadie would watch for their chance, leap at least five feet into the air, and knock the bat onto the floor. A bat on the floor is easy to sweep into the dustpan, so we appreciated their help. One time Sadie caught a bat in the middle of the night, brought it screeching into our bedroom, and deposited it in my husband's boot. It's a good thing we woke up and got rid of it because putting his foot into a bat boot the next morning probably would have given him a heart attack.

People who dislike cats claim that they are sneaky, territorial, finicky, unfriendly and aloof. Rufus and Sadie disproved all those stereotypes. When they curled up together, they looked like yin and yang. They ate from the same bowl with a synchronicity that was both amusing and remarkable. She'd lower her head to get food just as he raised his head to chew. There were no spats. They came when I whistled and ran to meet me when I came home from work. They liked to be carried at my shoulder like babies. They were compatible but not identical. Sadie had more spunk and Rufus was more affectionate.

I shouldn't claim favorites, but I will, and it was Rufus. When I was sick or cold or sad, he'd curl up with me and stay as long as I needed him. He liked to go out for walks, as long as I tucked him inside my coat. He liked to ride in the car, and he stood on the front seat and put his front paws on the dashboard whenever we approached the Dairy Queen, his favorite destination.

Because he had been a lost and starving kitten, Rufus never curbed his enthusiasm for any kind of food, so when I came home from work and discovered him lethargic and disinterested in eating one day, I was alarmed. I was six months pregnant with my first daughter, with my hormones in overdrive and tears poised to overtake me at all times. The vet checked him out that afternoon and suggested I leave Rufus overnight for tests. "I'm afraid Rufus might have leukemia," he said. He told me that the blood test results would be available the next day by 6.

I knew that feline leukemia is a fatal condition, and I had to take the next day off work because I couldn't pull myself together. I phoned the vet a couple of times to check on Rufus, but they could only tell me he was sleeping. My friends came to see me and couldn't believe what a sorry state I was in. When my husband came home from work, we drove to an appointment with our tax man, who asked questions about our deductions while I sat there sobbing and blowing my nose.

At 6 o'clock, I couldn't stand the tension or face the verdict. I asked my husband to make the call because I couldn't cope or even talk. As he dialed the number, the accountant looked on sympathetically and gravely. His look changed to disbelief when he heard the words, " Hello, my wife brought a cat in there yesterday......." I'm sure the accountant imagined far more serious reasons for my grief than a sick cat and thought I had lost my mind when he learned the truth. My mood changed to jubilation when the vet said Rufus was just fine and that we could pick him up on our way home.

Three months later, while I sat on my rocking chair timing contractions, Rufus sat on my lap--or what was left of it. A few days later both cats accepted their demotion when the baby assumed the role of the creature who needed attention. But babies grow, and in a few months Rufus and Sadie learned to keep their tails just out of reach as Jennifer crawled after them--her baby fingers reaching eagerly. They tolerated her drooling and pulling on their fur. Four years later when Susannah was born, they welcomed her into the fold.

No description of Rufus and Sadie would be complete without mentioning their many faults, which we tolerated.. Despite their elaborate climbing pole, they continued to destroy furniture. We tried training them with squirt guns, verbal commands and sprays. I read articles and tried techniques that worked for others. Both cats behaved as long as we watched them, but we'd come home and find evidence of misbehavior while we were out. We resorted to wrapping the couch with heavy quilts at night. It worked for a couple of days, but they figured out a way to increase their scratching pleasure by crawling inside the wrappings. As we drifted off to sleep, we'd hear, "rrrrrripppp" as Rufus and Sadie dragged themselves along the bottom of the couch.

Rufus was constantly on the watch for feeding opportunities. If someone got up from the dining room table to get something in the kitchen, he'd hop up on that person's chair, lower his head, and blindly reach one paw up to snag whatever might be on the plate. The kids kept watch and took pleasure in admonishing him, "Rufus, you blockhead, get down!" His most annoying behavior was his tendency to regard any open box, especially a guest's suitcase, as a litter box.

Rufus liked to sing along with Jacques Brel records. There was something about Brel's tunes and Flemish that aroused in Rufus a kindred spirit that inspired vocal expression. He would stand by the speaker and sing. He also liked to stroll up and down the piano keys at night.

He could open a door by pulling or pushing. I kept tampons in a nightstand that had a little door that closed with a click. Whenever the spirit moved him, Rufus would pull open the door and find himself a tampon, an invention that has all the features of a perfect cat toy--crackly paper on the outside, small size for a cat to carry, a rolling tube, and the grand prize if you can make your way through all those wrappings--a little cotton mouse with a string tail. I'd come home from work and discard whatever evidence I found, but sometimes I missed a few pieces. One time a man came to put insulation in the attic. When he pulled up a thick rug directly below the attic opening so that he could plant his step ladder, I heard him cry out, " Oh, my God!" I ran to the spot and discovered about a dozen tampons in a circle on the floor where the rug had been. How embarrassing! I bet he thought I suffered from some weird manifestation of PMS.

The kids wrapped catnip toys and put them under the Christmas tree, and Rufus would immediately find, unwrap, and destroy his toy. He didn't care about the toy; all he wanted was the catnip. I bought him a little gray mouse that looked like a piece of blackboard eraser with a string tail, and he loved to play with that. It was the closest thing to a tampon ever invented by cat toy manufacturers.

Sadie had her own list of eccentricities. She climbed Christmas trees and curled up in baskets of clean laundry. She loved to stand with her front paws in her water bucket. Whenever I brought groceries home, she invaded the bags to check everything out. She jumped onto impossibly high places. One time she jumped up to the cupboard and knocked over a gallon of milk I had just taken out of a grocery bag. When the plastic hit the floor, the bottle burst and milk filled the kitchen. I got so mad I chased her into the basement, where milk was dripping through the floorboards. The frightened kids kept yelling, " Run Sadie, Run!"

Both cats gave up naps when we started packing boxes prior to our California move, and I seriously worried that we might seal one of them in a crate. On the morning of the move, we locked them in a bedroom, which spooked Sadie so much that it was almost impossible to catch her and put her into the carrying case. Once captured, they both quieted down and rode across the country curled up together--catching up on lost sleep.

The first week in California, Rufus cut his foot on a nail. I found bloody footprints while rushing around trying to get the kids to school, and the tracks led to Rufus. I tried to practice damage control by putting him in the shower stall while one of us cleaned up the bloody house and the other checked the phone book for a nearby vet. He panicked in this unfamiliar environment, and by the time I got back to him, the shower stall looked like that famous scene from *Psycho*. My daughter wrapped his foot tightly and held him while I drove to the emergency vet.

When he was 16, Rufus started to show adverse signs of old age. First he started making caterwauling sounds, then he started going blind, and then he lost his hearing. Weary with age, he spent most days sleeping in the linen closet. His appetite remained strong, and he retained his sweet personality. He and Sadie still helped clean one another, and he chased his little mouse around the house for a minute or two every Sunday for old times' sake. Eventually he slowed down even more, and I started to help him out by carrying him downstairs to his litter box whenever I could.

One evening, shortly before Christmas, Rufus became very sick. The vet gave him intravenous fluids to combat dehydration but detected an orange-size mass in his abdomen. The girls ran out and bought him a Christmas present, hoping it would make him well, but I knew it was time to say goodbye to Rufus. I experienced additional grief when I had to drive him to the vet, take him out of his carrier, hand him over, and sign consent papers to administer the fatal dose. Throughout the ordeal, Rufus continued to purr, and I was so distraught that I couldn't bear to stay and hold him as he died--something I've always regretted. A couple of days later, I put the box containing his ashes in the linen closet where he spent his last weeks.

Sadie, who had been quite robust when her friend died, quickly started to lose weight and interest in life. A couple of months later, I found her near death huddled up against the bedroom wall. She died that night, presumably of a stroke.

We felt sad, but after losing Rufus, parting with his partner was less wrenching. Some folks throw in the towel after the death of a beloved pet and say, "Never again," but I agree with Ernest Hemmingway who said, " One cat just leads to another." We immediately got a couple of kittens and started the whole process again.

Pets help us to deal with the circle of life because they go from infancy to geriatrics in a few years, a reminder that nobody has an infinite amount of time to do whatever it is we think we want to accomplish. They help us practice patience, responsibility and tolerance so we know how to better deal with our fellow humans. But in addition to all that, I just like cats. They're quiet, soft, clean, and no matter how cluttered my office becomes, a cat can find a place to sit and keep me company. A stray animal is lucky to find a loving home, but the benefits are mutual. I don't think I'll ever be quite as attached to another pet as I was to Rufus and Sadie, but I will always be happy to share my life with a cat.

Rufus

Something Old, Something New,
Something Borrowed, Something Askew
by Esther Henderson Eaton

When a couple has been married fifty years, they are bound to have collected many wonderful memories, but as my husband Albert and I get ready to celebrate our Golden Anniversary, our wedding day still stands out as one of the best. Not everything went according to plans, but we all survived with our sense of humor intact.

We were married Thursday, August 20, 1953. I have no idea why we picked Thursday, but at that time nobody told us that a weekend wedding would be more practical. Since the wedding was scheduled for 9 a.m. at St. Joseph's church in the small town of Beroun, most out-of-town guests opted to stay two nights at a motel in nearby Pine City.

The wedding was beautiful with many friends, relatives and neighbors attending. After good wishes were extended and guests left the church, the wedding party decided to find a good place to eat breakfast. We wanted to stay out of the way of my folks, who were busily cooking an early afternoon dinner on the farm for thirty-some close relatives. We were all famished because we were Catholics who had fasted since midnight so that we could receive Holy Communion at the wedding Dressed as we were, however, in our fancy wedding outfits, we ruled out all available breakfast places and looked for something better. As we drove around unproductively, suddenly someone noticed that it was past noon, nearly time for dinner, so even though we hadn't eaten breakfast, we figured the guests of honor should hurry out to the farm to join the dinner guests. We didn't want to be late for our own celebration.

We were somewhat anxious, but as we drove into my folks' yard, we were relieved to find all the guests still sitting around. Apparently the food was not yet ready. We soon learned that dinner plans had hit a snag. With all the electricity used, the transformer in our yard had blown. My folks had taken the food to a neighbor's house about a quarter mile away so dinner would be a little late. Another neighbor, an electrician, had been called, and he supposedly had everything under control. Dinner would be served soon, we were told, even though the electrician was standing in the yard enjoying his second beer.

A bar was set up in the garage, and when dinner was finally served, no one seemed to notice. It took some effort to get their attention so they could finish dinner before folks started showing up for the reception.

Dinner had hardly been cleared when the reception that was scheduled from 2 till 6 for friends and neighbors began. The article in the local paper says that a hundred and fifty people attended. I really can't confirm that number, but I know there was never a dull moment. One of the highlights of the afternoon came when my 63 -year-old Uncle Ed and Al's 69-year-old Uncle Max decided to show the crowd how easy it was to stand on their heads. Although they were amazed, no other guests tried that trick. This was probably a good thing, because the women wore dresses.

Sometime around 7, when most of the crowd had left, Mother suggested I lie down and rest because we still had a wedding dance to attend. I refused because I didn't feel the least bit tired. Instead of resting, we spent most of the time before the dance getting the house in order after entertaining that large of a crowd.

The dance took place in a Pine City hall, and it was great fun. In those days there was a crazy custom or game in some social circles called kidnapping the bride, but nobody had told me about it. Around 11 p.m., my cousin Peggy appeared from nowhere and asked if I would go with her to the restroom. Of course I agreed. The restrooms were near the back door, and before we got that far, two of Albert's friends picked me up and away we went. They took me to the motel, where they had a room for the night. After a great amount of laughing and teasing, they phoned Albert at the dance and asked to speak to me.

Albert answered, "Just a minute; I'll get her."

They laughed and replied, "No you won't. We have her." After everyone had a good laugh, they picked Albert up, and soon we were all together back at the dance. By this time it was nearing 1 a.m. Friday morning. The dance ended, and it was time for everyone to go home.

When Albert and I got back to my folks' farm, we noticed that several of our friends had arrived before us, and we soon found out why. Albert's Ford coupe, painted with white shoe polish and decorated with toilet paper, was sitting up on four cement blocks with all four wheels off the ground. Although they were interested in eating any and all leftover food they could find in my folks' house, none of our friends seemed even slightly interested in helping us get that car off those blocks. Not only that, but they claimed they couldn't imagine who might have pulled such a dirty trick.

My mother had not attended the dance because she was too tired. She had fallen asleep and had not heard anyone messing around with Al's car, but a friend of hers who was spending the night watched the whole operation and debated whether or not she should wake my mom. Finally my dad went out and got the car ready to drive. The group of friends decided they had eaten their fill and had given us enough grief for one day. As they pulled away, my dad sat in Mom's kitchen rocker and laughed so hard I can still hear him.

As Dad rocked and laughed, Albert and I got ready to leave for our honeymoon. About a week earlier, Albert and I had stopped in Cambridge and made reservations to stay at a motel Thursday night. When we explained to the manager that we would be late, he gave us a key to the room and told us to let ourselves in any time we got there. By the time we arrived, it was about 3 a.m., and the key worked perfectly as we opened the door. But guess what? There was another couple in the bed! They weren't any happier to see us than we were to see them.

We woke the manager, who said he had forgotten about the arrangement he had made with us. Luckily he gave us a key to another room. The next morning, Albert realized that he had lost his wedding ring. We packed our bags and looked around the motel room, but we could not find the ring. We stopped at my parents' house and called the dance hall, all without success. Finally, when Albert was hanging up his wedding suit, the ring fell out of the pants leg cuff.

We left for the North Shore that afternoon. While eating dinner at a nice place at Port Arthur, I lost the gold filling from my front tooth. When we tried to go into the bar, the manager stopped me because they didn't admit women. We had planned to travel to Duluth, then on to Superior, but when we were about a half hour out of Port Arthur, Albert remembered that he had forgotten to pay the hotel bill, so we had to turn around and go back.   We stayed another night along the North Store and then went to Superior, where I found a dentist to fix my filling.

After a night in St. Croix, we returned to the farm, where our relatives gave us a food shower.   We loaded all our beautiful gifts into the car and headed off to our three room apartment in LeCenter.   In a few days, the new school year began, and Albert resumed his job as music teacher and I got a job in the school office.

Albert was 44 and I was 32 when we got married, and I guess our friends thought the occasion needed to be lively and fun.   Fate added a few crises and funny predicaments, and we passed the test by rolling with all the punches and having many good laughs afterwards.   Our first couple of days as husband and wife were so challenging that the next fifty years seemed like a piece of cake.

Esther Eaton, a retired Hennepin County Library clerk, grew up in Beroun. She lives in Bloomington with her husband Albert and enjoys reading, crocheting and visiting with her two adult daughters, Paula and Gloria.

Patricia Henderson, Esther Eaton, Albert Eaton, John Klosterman, August 20, 1953

The Mankato Flood of 1951
by Clayton Lagerquist

I can't think of a better place to grow up or a better time than Mankato, Minnesota, in the 30's and 40's--not only for the things we had, but for the things we didn't have. We didn't have traffic problems, crime, shootings, smog, drugs or gangs. We had the run of the town at all hours without worry.

These times were marked by the lack of change. No new houses were built, except for a few basement houses, which promised to be finished later. No new businesses were started, and none of the old ones failed. No new roads, bridges, or schools were built.

When millions of young men went off to war, their absence left a big void in the work force at home. Women, older men, and younger kids filled this void. We were expected to grow up faster than we ordinarily would have. Those who went to war became known as the greatest generation. Their kids born after the war became known as the baby boomers.

We were in between, and our generation had no identity. I guess we should be called the forgotten generation. In a way that's all right. We didn't seek notoriety or wish to change the world. We were industrious and well-behaved but independently minded. We thought we were entitled to an opinion, but didn't believe in civil disobedience as a tool to help us get our way. That came later, and we despised it.

During this time, when hardly anything changed except women's skirt lengths, Mother Nature taught us that not all things remain the same. I was looking forward to high school graduation so I could begin the next phase of my life. I assumed that it would come in a few weeks without problems just like everything else I had experienced. I was in for a shock.

No one expected the flood that hit Mankato and devastated North Mankato in 1951. The lowland near the river had flooded in previous years, but the high waters had not affected towns. That year, however, we had so much snow--88 inches-- that there was no place to put it. When the weather warmed up near the end of March, snow runoff combined with heavy rains caused the river to rise twelve feet in just three days.

The snow melted so fast that the Blue Earth River and the Minnesota River crested at the same time in Mankato. When things started to look bad, the call went out for volunteers to build a dike on McKinley Avenue at the north end of town. I took a shovel and went there intending to work for as long as it took to accomplish the job.

The Salvation Army was giving away cigarettes, gloves, and snacks, and the Red Cross was there selling the same things. The Municipal Building was set up for free meals so I went there to eat. I was standing in line waiting for a meal when someone asked me to put a Red Cross arm band on. I agreed, and watched as someone with a moving picture camera took our picture. I didn't realize it at the time, but we hometown workers were shown on TV as Red Cross workers who had come from someplace else to help.

We worked round the clock and managed to add more than two feet to the dike, but we were fighting an impossible force. On April 7, with the river rising at a rate of an inch per hour, the city engineer ordered families to evacuate their North Mankato homes.

I was working on the dike when someone noticed water coming down the street from the south. The river had already come through town and nobody was at the south end of town. We all left to go home to help rescue things in our houses.

I helped Dad carry things from the main floor to the second floor. As it turned out, that was a mistake because the first floor remained dry. We should have taken things out of the basement because all that was lost.

Dad loaded my mother, sister Ann, and dog Corky into the Buick and drove them to Minneapolis to stay with relatives. I was told to stay as long as I could to carry things upstairs and then drive my brother Bill's DeSoto over to high ground in Mankato.

Since Bill was in the Army, I considered the DeSoto to be mine. I was told to take the fan belt off so the fan wouldn't throw water on the distributor and kill the engine. It was a good thing I did, because it turned out that we were at a high point in town, and I had to drive through water that was higher than my tail pipe.

I got a room at the Saulpaugh Hotel. There was so much help needed on the Mankato side of the river that we worked days and nights. I helped evacuate people who lived near Sibley Park. I was riding on the back of a truck when some new helpers showed up. One was a classmate, Jerry Childs. He asked who we were evacuating, and I had to tell him that it was his folks.

I went back to North Mankato a couple of times with these trucks and saw one of our teachers, Mr. Fitterer, in hip boots pulling a small boat down the middle of Belgrade Avenue. The final quarter of my senior year of high school does not contain a more vivid memory.

Families were pretty disorganized, and radio announcers read lists of missing people. Actually, no lives were lost, but amid the chaos, people lost track of one another. My name was read once, but I didn't hear it. When my dad found me at the Saulpaugh Hotel, he wanted me to move to the Ben Pay, where he was staying. I went to pay for two nights, but the desk clerk told me I had only been there one night. I had lost track of days and nights while working round the clock.

The corner of Monroe and Center, North Mankato

The National Guard was called out, and they brought some amphibious vehicles called Ducks. When dignitaries like Governor Youngdahl showed up on April 10, they had a hard time controlling these Ducks in the strong current. They bumped into houses and knocked over mailboxes, adding to the damage. Eventually, however, the governor managed to funnel a significant amount of emergency cleanup relief and loans to flood victims.

At its height, flood water stood at over twenty-six feet. After April 10, the water started to recede slowly, but the effects of the flood were far from over. Many homes were ruined. Water had damaged possessions, and the threat of typhoid kept people from returning to homes with polluted water standing in basements. The Army lent the town dozens of pumps, but cleanup would take months. We had to stay out of our house for several weeks, and access to North Mankato was controlled.

Amidst all the work, we found a few social outlets. I went to a dance with Julie Williams, and I had to get some proper clothes from the house. I got a permit and went to our house to get one of my dad's suits because I didn't have a suit. The power was off, and I couldn't see very well in his closet.

I found one of Dad's oldest suits, which was fine with me, but the pants were about four inches too big around the middle. I decided I could fold the pants over and hide the gaping waist with the suit coat, but this was not as easy as I hoped.

Julie's mother had a gathering at her house for a few of Julie's friends and their dates before the dance. It was warm in the house, and she wanted me to take my coat off. I refused, but she could see that I was uncomfortable.

Occasional recreational and social breaks did not mean that our civic responsibility for dealing with the flood's aftermath had ended. Cleanup after floodwaters receded was the worst part of the ordeal. Our basement not only filled with water, but the floor heaved and water came in along with a dump truck full of silt.

I know how much silt it was, because it all came from under our garage, and it took that much sand to fill the hole. We didn't know about the hole until I noted that there was no dirt in the floor drain. I put a rake handle into the hole to see how deep the hole was, and the handle couldn't reach the bottom. There were holes like that in a lot of places throughout the town. The *Mankato Free Press* ran a picture of a road grader that had been swallowed by one such hole, and the top of the grader was even with the street.

Cleanup work was heavy and difficult. I remember trying to help my dad carry a heavy soaked mattress up the stairs. We tried to shovel silt out a basement window, but it was too heavy. Bill Tanley came by and told my dad he would bring a lift pump for him. With the pump we could use city water to hose the silt into the pump, and the slurry would be carried to the street. The city water was not potable because it was so heavily chlorinated that we were able to use it as a disinfectant.

In spite of all we did to help save our town and our homes, the boys my age did not achieve any special social identity or accolades after the flood of 1951. The flood marked an end to the last vestiges of my childhood--my Boy Scout activities, my job at the drug store, and even my high school days. I graduated from Mankato High School in the Class of 1951 without attending most of that last quarter's classes, but what I learned during the flood and its aftermath could not be learned in classes or books. The flood forced me to grow up a little more and marked the end to a lot of things, but my experiences cemented my belief that there was no better place to grow up in those days than Mankato, Minnesota.

Clayton Lagerquist retired in 1993 after 37 years in radiological physics, including 7 years at the University of Minnesota. He and his wife of 47 years divide their time between Colorado and Minnesota. They have four children and six grandchildren.

Before I Was 8
by Lloyd Deuel

The Foreston community leaders decreed that kids under 8 years old, or those who had not started third grade, were not to be expected to milk cows. They believed that little children needed sleep more than their fathers needed help with milking. Although this policy imposed some hardship on farm fathers who could always use an extra hand with chores, the community accepted its wisdom and enforced it by peer pressure. Though some said that the local boys were being coddled, my mom and dad, Ira and Esther Deuel, respected and followed this rule.

I was born in Foreston in 1929, and shortly thereafter we moved to the old Deuel farm about five miles south of Foreston. My early childhood was a happy time that I remember fondly. Although I have a few preschool memories of summer barn dances and a few other events, my most vivid memories begin about the time I started school.

When I came home from the first day of kindergarten in April of 1935, my parents wanted to know all about it. The most important thing I told them was that I was the only boy in school who didn't have a jack knife, and I really needed one. That evening my dad took me to the Estes Brook General Store, which was about the most interesting store a little boy could visit. Visiting the store with my dad was especially exciting because it was unlikely that he'd make me try on clothes.

We met my classmate Wilfred Totzke and his dad Bill. Bill and my dad soon got into this talk about the "only boy in school who didn't have a jack knife." They dragged that one back and forth until Wilfred and I thought they'd never quit. Finally they turned their attention to the knife display. To our delight, they didn't examine the cheap ones but went right to the 25 cent knives. Wilfred and I couldn't read the prices yet, but we knew the difference. The hard part was that we had to promise our dads that we wouldn't sharpen our knives, but that we'd wait for our dads to do that. We waited a long time. We had to promise to keep other rules too, and in those days a promise was a promise.

My cousin Bud Bemis had a Shetland pony that his uncle Charlie had bought for him. That pony was the envy of every boy in three school districts. I let my dad know my feelings about the pony, and one day Dad brought a goat home for me. This was a huge goat as goats go. He was white, no horns, no objectionable odor, weighed 250 pounds and was very strong. I could ride him, harness him to a wagon or sled that my dad built, or just lead him around. He was gentle and my constant companion.

Unfortunately the goat would eat anything, and he would go to great lengths to get food he wanted. My mom would bake bread or cookies and put them on a kitchen counter to cool and then leave the house. The darn goat would get the screen door open and walk into our house and take a loaf of bread or whatever in his mouth and run outdoors with it. It seemed my mom was chasing that goat with her broom quite a bit.

When I started school, a neighbor kid, Willard Smith, would come over every morning and give me a ride to school on his bike. One morning Willard came into our house to wait while my mom finished packing my lunch. We heard glass break on the porch and opened the door just in time to see the goat finishing Willard's home canned peaches that his mother sent in a glass jar. The goat had already eaten three sandwiches made from six slices of homemade bread, some cookies, and a cake when he rolled the glass jar off the porch and ate the peaches without getting any broken glass in his mouth. All that was left was the spoon. My mom was very ticked off at that darn goat. She had to make Willard another lunch and then call Willard's mom to explain the situation. We were on a party line, and in short order everyone in School District #6 knew all about the incident, and it made their day. The goat was high on my mom's hate list for quite a while.

The premiere entertainment event of the school year was the District #6 school Christmas program. The whole community packed into the school, and the kids worked hard to ensure that nobody went away disappointed. One year, however, the attendees got more than they bargained for. About two or three weeks after the program, everyone in the area came down with the mumps at the same time.

Dad had already had the disease, but Mom got sick. Dad built a cot for me in the kitchen, took on all kitchen responsibilities, and brought Mom all her meals. I never did get sick. I don't think we ever saw a doctor, but by telephone Mrs. Clara Northway kept everyone in touch.

Those who were not sick pitched in to help their neighbors with farm chores.   Everyone divided up the work the best they could, and it was my dad's task to help the Axt and Northway families.   Each morning my dad would start our stoves and then go to the barn and milk and feed our cows.   Then he would come in and get me up and cook breakfast for Mom and me.   We would then go to the barn and take care of the pigs.   I would tend to my goat, and he would harness our horses and hook them up to the bobsled, and we'd head for the Axt farm.

Jessie Axt was the only person at that farm who didn't have mumps. She would start milking, and my dad would finish up.   Then he would get hay from the haymow for that morning and extra for night chores.   After he fed and watered all their stock, he would clean out the barn.   In the meantime, my job was to gather eggs and take care of the chickens and pigs.   When I finished those chores, I carried stove wood and piled it on their back porch.   My dad told me how high the stack should be to last two days in case I missed a day.   It was really cold, but I had to stay out of their house.   I was supposed to warm up and   rest in the barn--where Dad could check on me, and I could only talk to the Axt boys through the kitchen window.

After finishing at the Axt farm, we would hook up to the sled and go to the Northway farm, where two people were mumps-free, Mrs. Northway and her daughter Clara.   By the time we arrived, they had finished milking, and my dad would feed and water their stock and clean their barn.   He would take advantage of daylight to get hay down for two feedings because there were no lights upstairs in barns for evening chores.

Watering farm animals was quite a chore with no running water. Some farmers chopped holes in the creek ice if it wasn't too thick, but most of the time getting water involved hand pumping or starting up a gasoline engine.   There was lots of carrying water by hand.   I gathered eggs and fed the chickens and pigs and stacked firewood like I did at the Axt farm.   And of course, I talked to the Northway kids through their kitchen window.   I was not allowed to help Dad with the milking because I was too young.

When we finally got home, my dad would clean his own barn and finish taking care of his own chores.   He would then come to the house and fix dinner for Mom and me.   While he milked the cows, I washed dishes and reported to Mom, through closed doors, just how we had spent our morning.

After this I had to do the wood bit for our house and take care of my goat.   My dad would hook up the horses again, and we would set out to do afternoon chores for our neighbors.   My dad would have to crank the cream separator at each farm to save the cream to be sold later.   It would be dark before we called it a day, and my dad would fix supper for us.   I seemed just barely able to make my 8 o'clock bedtime.

One of our neighbors collected all the cream and took it by horse and sled to Foreston, where it was sold.   On his way back, he would deliver whatever groceries were needed on each farm.   I've thought about this arrangement through the years, and I now appreciate just how tough my dad was to be able to put in such long, hard days.   In those days it was a common practice to help friends and neighbors, even if it meant you had to make sacrifices.

School was closed for three weeks during the mumps siege, but eventually things returned to normal.   It was a cold winter with a lot of snow.   There was no electric power, radio, or television, and entertainment was limited to whatever we could do ourselves.   Mom and Dad were cribbage players, and they decided to teach the young people in the neighborhood to play cribbage.   My dad made six cribbage boards and they invited older kids to ski over to our house and play cribbage twice a week.   They would serve big bowls of popcorn, and everyone seemed to have a good time.   I enjoyed having so many interesting people in our house and hoped unsuccessfully for a reprieve of my 8 o'clock bedtime.

In the spring, our neighbors the Northways were inundated with rats, which were so numerous that they became a threat to the chickens. The oldest Northway boy, Llewellyn, asked my dad to come over to their farm one evenings and help shoot rats.   Ira Deuel had the reputation for having no peer in marksmanship.   The next morning he mentioned that the rat posse had been successful and that they would begin to gather up the carcasses when it became light enough to see.   He also predicted that the rats would replenish their population, despite their death toll.

I left for school a little early that morning. Normally I took a shortcut across their meadow and through their yard so I could walk to school with the Northway kids. This morning, Reuben had gathered a pile of about eighty dead rats and had a few more places to check to try to reach a total of ninety. He had a pile of branches and old scrap lumber that he was going to use to build a rat funeral pyre.

The Northways were the kind of kids who would always share what they had. When farm boys found a dead rabbit or crow, they would look for a stick to poke it and turn it over with because many little interesting critters often crawled beneath the dead animal. Now some of my school chums took the attitude of finders keepers and wouldn't share something like that, but Reuben Northway would always share what he found with me.

Reuben offered to let me help look for more rats. While he was talking, I looked at the pile of rats. A pile of eighty dead rats is quite impressive. It seemed I could see some of them move. As I edged my way sideways around the pile while Reuben recited his plan, dozens of rat eyes seemed to be watching me. I finally made the excuse that I was going to school early and would have to miss the big bonfire.

I didn't have a good day at school. When I walked home with the Northway kids, I didn't cut through their yard and take my usual shortcut. In fact, I stayed on the road and avoided looking in their yard where the fire had burned.

I dreaded my 8 o'clock bedtime because I imagined what my night would be like, and I was right. I could see rat eyes every time I closed my eyes. I could see rats crawling and rats hiding, and they were not happy rats. The next morning I started a ritual that I followed for quite awhile. I would crawl over and check the far side of my bed and then the floor on the side where I got out of bed. A fellow just couldn't be too sure what was down there waiting to bite his bare feet.

In April of 1937, my parents decided to have an auction and move to Foreston. This was a traumatic move for all concerned. All of our farm animals had to be sold except our stallion Jerome and my goat, which were to be kept in Grandpa Deuel's stable in town. This arrangement didn't work out for the goat.   My dad told me that there were just too many kids who wanted to ride him, and that it wasn't fair to the animal. He asked the Northways if they would keep him for the rest of his days, and they agreed.

A very strange thing happened.   All the rats on the Northway farm left the premises a short time after the goat arrived.   This goat was no threat to the rats as far as anyone could determine, but the rats and that goat were not compatible.   After thinking about it, the adults concluded that while the goat lived on our farm, we had no rats either.   So despite his bad habit of stealing food, the goat turned out to be more of an asset than a liability.   I quit dreaming about rats too.

After listening to third graders brag about how many cows they had to milk before going to school, I had been looking forward to assuming that responsibility.   But I was still a 7-year-old second grader when we moved to Foreston--too young to milk cows, according to local policy. As a result, I didn't learn to milk a cow.   In fact, I have never milked a cow.   And I've never before told anyone about that dark hole in my life--until now.

Lloyd Deuel is a retired machinist who lives in Brooklyn Center with his wife Phyllis. They enjoy gardening, woodworking and retirement.

Berniece Pennington: The First Miss Minnesota
by Rosemary Wulff

I grew up on a farm north of Rochester along a quiet county road that is now Highway 52. As the youngest daughter in a family of eight children, I looked to my oldest sister Berniece for guidance and companionship.

Berniece found my name in a book she was reading and convinced my mother to name me Rosemary instead of Lucille. She was 12 years old when I was born--old enough to help my mother take care of a baby sister, and perhaps this special dependency helped create the bond that I still feel. She was an unusually lovely person, both in appearance and demeanor, and we were very close despite our age difference.

When Berniece was 17, some State Fair officials who were visiting my father were so charmed by her beauty that they asked her to be the first Miss Minnesota. My parents discussed the invitation, and after much controversy, they finally agreed to allow Berniece to accept this opportunity.

That fall my parents and Berniece were honored guests at the State Fair in St. Paul. They sat in a grandstand box to watch festivities, and Berniece accepted a gift from the governor and flowers from State Fair officials. She enjoyed a grand tour of the Twin Cities. In those days, such adventures were unusual for a farm girl from Rochester. Berniece must have felt like Cinderella, and as the little sister, I shared her joy.

After she graduated from high school the next year, Berniece entered Rochester Junior College. We shared a room, and I loved to have Berniece read to me every night. Sometimes we studied and admired the brochures from Macalester that she had sent for. Berniece wanted to attend Macalester after junior college.

One November morning, our Aunt Della knocked on our bedroom door, and without a word Berniece sprang out of bed and followed her downstairs. I ran to the other kids' bedrooms and told them what had happened, and we all came out into the hall and leaned over the stair railing. I remember saying, "I smell a doctor." An hour or so later, Aunt Della asked us to come see our new baby brother. As I entered the room and saw the white uniform of the nurse who had accompanied the doctor, I asked her where her wings were. I was sure that she was an angel who had brought my baby brother from heaven.

A few weeks after that, Berniece was taken to the hospital with a burst appendix. Although she survived, the doctors discovered that she had tuberculosis of the stomach. We drank unpasteurized milk at that time, and doctors now know that an infected cow can transmit tubercle bacillus through its milk. I'm not sure that's how she contracted the disease, but it's a possibility.

Tuberculosis was the worst sentence that the doctors could have pronounced. Although some people recovered on their own, no medicines were available to combat the disease, and the disease almost invariably led to a slow and painful death. Because tuberculosis was thought to be very contagious to a new baby and other children, there was no thought that Berniece could return home. She was sent to Mineral Springs Sanatorium in Cannon Falls, where she was put in a ward with patients who had tuberculosis of the lung, and eventually her lungs also became infected.

Berniece remained at Mineral Springs for the next eight years, a virtual prisoner. We visited her every other Sunday, a difficult trip on a bad road during winter, and many times our car broke down on the way. Children were not allowed inside the sanatorium, so I was only able to talk to Berniece when she came to the third floor window.

The only therapy available in the 30's was fresh air and sunshine so Berniece had to spend long hours in bed on the screened porch. She found it difficult to write letters because her hands were so cold, but she did manage to write regularly. We read her letters and then thoroughly washed our hands because the common belief was that TB was fiercely communicable. I think my mother had to burn the letters as a precaution against the disease.

Berniece must have felt like a leper, unable to know the touch of loved ones and afraid that she might transmit the disease to her siblings.

Since she was an affectionate person, she must have been miserable from this lack of human contact. We now know that those severe precautions that prevented human contact for anyone with tuberculosis were unnecessary, and it still makes me tearful to think how many ways my sister suffered. I'm sure she would have gladly traded her few moments of glory as the first Miss Minnesota for a life as a healthy person.

There is no happy ending to this story. Berniece died December 22, 1933, at the age of 25. My mother gave me a diary that Christmas, and for many years I wrote letters to Berniece in it.

Her memory has influenced my life in so many ways. I kept her Macalester brochures, and years later I graduated from the college she had dreamed of attending. While there, I met my wonderful husband and father of my five children. Although I wish often that I could have shared the many joys and milestones of my life with Berniece over the years, I'm sure she was looking over my shoulder.

Bernice Pennington
Miss Minnesota of 1925

Rosemary Wulff worked as a medical technician in Albert Lea. She has five chidren and ten grandchildren.

Grandpa John Mason Peterson
by Edmund John Peterson

Grandpa John was my father's widowed father who lived with us. He had no middle name but was known as John Mason Peterson because he had worked as a stone mason. In those days, grandpas were always old. It was hard for me and my older sisters Vivien and Rose to imagine grandpa as ever being young. What a strange baby he must have been with his mustache and goatee!

Bent by years, Grandpa was a man of average height and swarthy complexion. He had a high forehead, sunken cheeks, and he prided himself on his mustache and goatee, which he kept neatly trimmed. A few strands of grayish black hair valiantly tried but failed to cover his balding pate. Toothless, Grandpa gummed his food and was able to chew everything except corn on the cob. He sliced off the kernels and closed his eyes as he savored their succulent goodness.

To sneak into Grandpa's room was a delight. His chewing tobacco came in a colorful wrapper that looked like a thin candy bar. Once I pinched off a bit and slipped it under my tongue. Wow! It was my first and last chaw. Grandpa's room contained many mysterious little boxes and treasures. A padlocked trunk that he brought from Sweden stood in one corner. On the bureau was a collection of rocks and post cards from Colorado, where he had gone to seek relief from the bronchial asthma he battled all his life.

When Grandpa's wheezing got heavy, he would get out his pie tin and shake some powder out of a blue tin container into a neat little mound. Then he would light the stuff and inhale the fumes through a long funnel shaped cone he had made. In mild weather, Grandpa smoked this foul smelling concoction outside. When it was too cold outdoors, he smoked indoors, and our house reeked with a penetrating, acrid odor for hours.

Once my uncle Hjalmer gave Grandpa one of his Lucky Strike cigarettes to see if smoking would help his condition. Grandpa sat on the front porch steps drawing on the weed with eyes tightly shut. We laughed to see our stern old grandpa, of all people, smoking a modern cigarette.

The cigarette did nothing but aggravate his wheezing, however, so it was back to the powder, cone, and pie tin.

Often in the evening after supper, our family observed family prayers. Invariably Grandpa's prayers were interminably long and in Swedish, a language we children understood only when our parents used it to talk about us.

Grandpa was a fine Christian gent, but he was also human. Everyone was excited when the Sears Roebuck catalog arrived in the mail. Grandpa, the clan patriarch, got it first. The pages devoted to women's corsets and underwear held a special fascination for him. Being a late bloomer, I never understood why he didn't focus his attention on the toy section.

Sex was never discussed in our house. It was generally understood that the stork had brought the babies. But there was one book written in Swedish that Grandpa used to read. It must have been an anatomy book or a sex guide because it featured graphic drawings of men and women. One day I innocently picked it up and started paging through it. My mother turned red and snatched it away from me. When I asked if I could see the book again, she said she had burned it because it was not for children.

More saint than sinner, Grandpa would sit under the shade tree and recite the psalms in Swedish. Grandpa spoke very little English. When he'd watch us kids play on weekends, he'd laugh and say, "Saturday, Sport Day." And recalling his youth in Sweden he'd add, "I see you on the school house ground for fifty year ago!"

Our neighbor, Bernice Wilkins, had a pet dog named Sis that was a constant irritation to Grandpa. Sis was a scrap of a dog with uncertain lineage. Her whiskers were always brown from digging in the garbage. Bernice loved that miserable mutt as much as Grandpa detested it. Sis would invade our garden, which was Grandpa's domain. Being a Christian gentleman, Grandpa couldn't do much about the situation except embarrass Bernice when she came around with Sis. Mustering his best English, he would mutter, "Ha ha ha. The five cent dog. I give you five cents for the dog." Bernice shook her head gravely. She wouldn't take a million dollars for that pathetic creature.

Our drinking water came from a well that was located about thirty feet from our back door.   Rain water was collected off the roof and piped into the cistern and was pumped back up with a small hand pump in the kitchen.   This soft water was used for washing and bathing but was not suitable for drinking.   Our drinking water was hard and full of iron.   It was good water, but you had to acquire a taste for it, and it always left a red sediment in the bottoms of glasses.   In below zero weather, the outside pump that produced the drinking water always froze up.   Our neighbors, the Wilkins, shared the pump with us.

Mr. Wilkins' father, whom we called " Lila Guban"(Swedish for little man) because of his small stature, used to come over to fetch water.   Often in the winter he'd knock on our door and ask for the tea kettle, which was always steaming on the kitchen's wood-burning range.   He'd have to use the boiling water to thaw the pump.   Great clouds of steam ascended into the air before the pump burped to life.   When Lila Guban returned the kettle, he'd have frost in his mustache.   Since he was of my grandpa's generation, you'd think the two would have been friends, but Mr. Wilkins wasn't Swedish so the two men didn't speak the same language.

A very resourceful man, Grandpa mended his own clothes and was a capable carpenter and gardener.   He had little formal education but enjoyed reading his Swedish books, and he wrote with a beautiful, flourishing hand.   He was dapper, and he kept his things orderly.   If he had a fault, it was his aversion to bathing.   While we were expected to comply with mother's directive to take baths every Saturday night, our mother would have to sell Grandpa on the idea every six weeks or so.   When he eventually took his turn in the old tin tub, he would concede that taking a bath was a good idea.   Thanking my mother for talking him into the experience, he would say, "Tak fir badet!" and march off to bed.

During the Depression, Grandpa spent his summers in our town of Buffalo and his winters in Minneapolis with his son Lenis.   Grandpa was always an early riser, but on the morning of the day when he was to migrate to Minneapolis, he was up early to await the arrival of Lenis.

No monarch looked more regal than our grandpa as he sat dressed in his Sunday best alongside his packed suitcases awaiting his chauffeur.   Grandpa wore a great fur coat he called a pels, and matching fur hat.   When

Lenis came to pick him up, he would help Grandpa into the pels. Grandpa would give a little laugh, and into the Chevrolet he would go.

Grandpa tolerated city life, but his heart was in the country. With the arrival of the first spring robin, he would return to our house. Perhaps my mother enjoyed his winter vacation more than he did. I'm sure she didn't miss supervising his baths and washing his heavy woolen underwear by hand, since she had no washing machine. Summers gave Grandpa a chance to help with the garden and to go out and exercise his independence.

July Fourth was a special day when I was a boy, the one day when we could count on having homemade ice cream. It was my job to turn the crank of the ice cream freezer, which consisted of a metal container in a wooden bucket. Ice and salt were packed all around this canister. When the ice cream was frozen, the dasher was removed, and it was my good fortune to lick it clean. What a sweet reward! Along with legal fireworks and ice cream, another standard feature of the 4th of July was observing Grandpa. He would emerge from his room dressed in a black coat, white vest and neatly pressed trousers. Cane in hand, he would walk across town to the old conference grounds of the Evangelical Free Church in Franson Park and spend the day in the courts of the Lord.

Although generally healthy, Grandpa was subject to what we called his spells. While dining at the table, his face would turn beet red and he would begin to shake. My dad would shout, "Far Far!" (Swedish for father) and shake him. In about a minute, he would recover his hearty laugh and resume eating.

Despite asthma, spells, and lack of baths, Grandpa John lived to be 86. He spent the last few years of his life in his old family home on Tower Hill in Buffalo with his son Hjalmer and daughter-in-law Cornelia, who later bought the home from the family estate.

Our beloved Grandpa John died in his bedroom in that house after a brief illness and a bath given by his daughter Ethyle, a registered nurse in Minneapolis. While she was at it, Ethyle shaved off his goatee. And so it was that Ethyle saw to it that Grandpa John was dispatched clean and shorn to meet his maker.

Grandpa John lay in state in the old family parlor, as was the custom in those days. When we came to pay our respects, we saw Grandpa John reposing regally in a gray cloth covered casket, wearing his familiar Sunday suit, sanitized, freshly shaved, his mustache neatly trimmed. And miracle of miracles--there was his goatee, restored to its original splendor. The mortician who knew Grandpa, laboriously, whisker-by-whisker, re-goateed Grandpa. "It just wouldn't be Mr. Peterson without that goatee," observed the mortician. Our family greatly appreciated the restoration.

After the home wake, Grandpa's body was moved to the little brick Swedish Mission Church he helped build with his strong and faithful hands. After the church service, he was laid to rest in the old Swedish Mission Cemetery outside Buffalo.

The John Mason Peterson family circa 1900. Top: Hjalmar, Lenis, Hulds, Gideon, Emrls. Bottom: John (minus his goatee) Ethyle, Jenny, Elsie, Edna and Karin.

Grandpa John was a stern but good man, a true pioneer. There are several monuments to his skill as a mason around Buffalo. He built the stone wall in front of the Ebenezer Home on Lake Boulevard. His nine children have all died. My sister and I, along with a California cousin, are the last of his seven grandchildren. John Mason Peterson had thirteen great grand-children and lots of great-great-grandchildren so part of him lives on in some way. Grandpa John is gone, but you can't kill the Petersons. Minnesota, after all, is the land of 10,000 Petersons.

Edmond John Peterson, a former mortician, raised four children in St. Paul and retired to Chisago County. He and his wife live in Lindstrom. He wrote this story at the encouragement of all the great grandchildren.

Strong Hands
by Dex Westrum

My father was a professional golfer, an amateur hockey player, and a standout high school football halfback. I was none of those things. In high school, I was starting tackle on the football team, a semi-regular on the wrestling team, and on the golf course I could break 80 every once in a while. I was a passable athlete, but I wasn't like my father.

When I became a father for the first time just a few weeks short of my 54th birthday, my first thoughts were about sports. I was happy to see that my son Clayton had long fingers (like Linda, his mother). Most of the tournament caliber golfers I have met have long fingers. Strong, long fingers provide more flexible control of the club and more acceleration through the swing. Should he become consumed by the game like my father, Clayton will be equipped with two of the essential tools--good hands.

Clayton is named after the best golfer in our family, my uncle Bumper. Most people who know my uncle in Albert Lea or in Rochester where he was director of golf for the city don't know that his name is Clayton, so it isn't as if my Clayton were all set to ride on my uncle's reputation. Bumper, the sixth of seven children, got his nickname because as an infant he kept running into things and bumping his head. His older siblings, who didn't see how he would make it out of infancy, thought he was clumsy, yet he grew to be the most coordinated of the lot.

Bumper Westrum

He played first man on the Albert Lea High School golf team when he was in sixth grade. He was state high school golf champion in 1950 and 1952. As a senior, he was drafted by the football coach to punt and kick extra points because the team didn't have a kicker. Bumper wasn't crazy about playing football, so he made a deal. He would show up and kick if he didn't have to practice. He set high school records in basketball and played on a semi-pro team, The Vagabonds.

The Vagabonds traveled around the country playing local teams and putting on exhibitions. Once in a while they were booked against their prototype, The Harlem Globetrotters. The first time he played the Globetrotters, Bumper stole the ball from Goose Tatum during one of his routines. The crowd loved it. They stomped and cheered. Tatum wasn't used to playing against people who could outfox him. At half time, he came over to Bumper and said, "Don't ever do that again, kid. The people pay to see me, not you."

My dad and all of his brothers except Bumper had sturdy, burly, solid builds. Bumper was skinny. Clayton clearly has my family build. He has a big torso and is already a chunk. When people see him, they recognize him as a potential athlete and talk about how he will be good at whatever their own favorite sport is. Having a son who is a good athlete would be nice, but I have a deeper wish for Clayton. All my life I have felt a great loss because I am not musical. I can't play anything. When I see Clayton's long fingers, I hope that he will be a pianist, that he will bring out the music all humans are supposed to have inside them.

My hope that Clayton will be musical is not far fetched. My father's father played numerous instruments, most notably the bugle. He was American Legion national champion many times and played taps for every veteran who was ever buried in the old hometown. Grandpa had all kinds of horns that hung on the wall of his porch--one of them was six feet long. I remember him practicing the bugle all the time, usually on the porch.

I think it would be nice if Clayton played music because my grandfather had seven kids and not one of them was interested in playing an instrument. In fact, he had wished to have a family band, but all his children wanted to play was sports. Grandpa not only played music, but also wrote poetry, the kind that rhymes; a lot of his poems were published in The *Evening Tribune*. Most of the time Grandpa was a quiet man who sat in his chair in the living room on Abbot Street and smoked his pipe.

Grandpa Gustav Westrum

I always thought it strange that a man who was so pacific and so pensive would have children who appeared not at all reflective but intensely physical, always taking life on concrete terms. In fact, more than one of my friends has suggested that my grandparents raised feral children. I don't know that I would go so far as to say that, but I do know that Grandpa and Grandma were not systematic parents. They didn't believe in doctors, for example. My father had rheumatic fever when he was 10. My great aunt Murt was visiting, thought something was wrong, and took him to the doctor. Uncle Bumper was told by Army doctors that he had once had polio, probably as a teenager. He remembers a year when he missed a lot of golf matches because his shoulder was always sore, but nobody ever told him he should find out why it ached.

I don't think my grandparents thought discipline was very important. One of my favorite stories is about the night Grandpa was practicing the bugle on his porch and all of a sudden my dad, then a high school kid, burst through the door and beat it up stairs. A few minutes later, Big Ole, the future chief but then just a beat cop like Grandpa, appeared. "Gus," he said. "Have you seen Lyle? There was a hell of a row down on Dunham Street, and I think he was mixed up in it." Grandpa set his bugle on his knee and said, "He's upstairs asleep. He wasn't feeling well and hasn't been out of the house." And that was the end of it.

My dad and his siblings always went pretty much their own ways. But I don't know that anyone should blame their parents. Maybe they were just strong willed people. In the forty-five or so years that I had my father, I pretty much came to the conclusion that not much can be done to change the behavior of a strong-willed person.

But now I am the dad, and Clayton is a strong-willed person. A lot can be said for strong-willed people. In the best scenario, Clayton should be able to follow through on the desires of his heart rather than require others to get him what he wants. And Grandpa was not totally passive. He was a boxing champion in the Navy. Maybe his plan as a father was to stay out of his children's way, allowing them to discover their own paths and take care of themselves.

Dex Westrum is a graduate of Albert Lea High School. He teaches literature and film at the Milwaukee Center of Upper Iowa University.

Memories of the College of St. Teresa
by Sister Mary Lonan Reilly, OSF

I was 20 years old when I came to the College of St. Teresa as a postulant with the Sisters of St. Francis. Although I had earned some college credits and had taught for two terms in a rural school, I was quite overwhelmed by the extent of the campus and the beauty of the surrounding area. I had come from a thinly populated farm community on the plains of central South Dakota, an area that I had grown to love, but which provided an entirely different landscape from that of Winona.

At first I felt homesick for the brilliant sunrises and sunsets and the wide open spaces that had been such a part of my childhood and young adulthood. I found it difficult to relate to one of my classmates, already a college graduate, who declared that if she could spend the rest of her life on the campus, she would be completely happy. However, I soon adjusted to the new environment, and by the time Christmas vacation arrived, I regretted that my time would be spent at the Mother House in Rochester.

The following year I entered the Novitiate, and later I was sent out to teach junior high history in Chicago, Austin St. Augustine, Caledonia, Winona Cathedral and Wilmont. Finally I moved up to high school teaching at Cotter in Winona.

During those years, I attended a number of summer sessions, which I anticipated not only for the knowledge to be gained but also for the reunion of classmates and mission sisters. Classes were demanding, and all the younger sisters had work charges as well. But evenings and weekends provided leisure and cultural opportunities. There were musical and dance programs, Winona Summer Theater stage plays in the St. Cecilia Auditorium, and formal dinners and celebrations. Picnics on St. Michael's field and later on the concourse between resident buildings were always on the summer agenda. And those so inclined played softball, volleyball, or tennis. We strolled along the sidewalks in twos and threes and relaxed around the swimming pool in the lower level of Lourde's Hall.

After several years I was notified by the Mother Superior of the Franciscan congregation that I would begin study for an advanced degree in history at Notre Dame, and this assignment produced ambivalent feelings. I welcomed the opportunity for additional study and the experience of being on a university campus with other scholars, but I knew I would miss working with junior high students and living in a small community in a convent setting. Did I really want to exchange that for a position at the college? In those days I really had little to say in the matter, so I obediently enrolled at the University of Notre Dame. I was pleasantly surprised to find out how this experience broadened and enriched my life.

In the fall semester of 1969, I began teaching at the College of St. Teresa, a job that continued for eleven years. During this time so many fine young women touched my life and challenged my ability to meet their needs. A student who had lost her hearing registered for one of my classes. How would I reach her and still do justice to the large group? Her enrollment and success marked the first time a deaf student had attended the college. Because of a generous classmate who duplicated notes, tutored her, and previewed materials so that she could participate in class discussions, she persevered and produced a fine term paper. This is just one example of the generosity and helpfulness I experienced while interacting with hundreds of Teresans.

Committee involvements and team teaching enhanced my academic background. A humanities course based on *Don Quixote*, taught with a Spanish Department professor turned out to be a memorable venture, and I learned as much or more than the students.

Student activities were abundant. Celebrations were vibrant and long-treasured. The Night of 1001, beginning with an all-school family dinner, followed by Liturgy of Lights, then Senior Caroling, and finally donuts and hot chocolate was an eagerly anticipated holiday tradition. Choice of Campus Court members and the pageantry surrounding their announcement and installation was another event that brought most of the community to the main court in front of Lourdes Hall.

Spiritual opportunities were ample, and Sunday liturgies--often with accompaniment by student musicians--were well-planned and attended by sisters and students. We often got together with the Sisters of Alverna Hall and with others who lived at St. Anne Hospice, Tau Center, or elsewhere. During this time my love for the college, previously deeply rooted, blossomed and matured.

After six years, I stopped teaching and moved into an administrative position as the executive assistant to the college president. Classroom responsibilities were replaced with committee work, accreditation reports, and planning graduation ceremonies. All were fulfilling because they were challenging and appreciated. The college community had truly become my home and family.

College of St. Teresa graduation, 1977

In 1977, when the college announced plans to close, I was devastated and heartbroken. Fortunately I was able to find a similar institution that provided new challenges and friendships. But when I returned to Minnesota, it was natural that I contacted those who were promoting the CSTea House Inc., an alumnae office located where the old Tea House used to be.

Through the many endeavors of these and other Teresan groups, and by the very lives of all our graduates, I believe that CST lives today in a new way, one that continues to unite us as loyal Teresans celebrating together as we recall our past and professing while singing our Alma Mater that "Our love for thee will ne'er grow old." I thank God that many of the more than 8000 Teresans living among us today have contributed both to that past and to the rebirth that has emerged.

Sister Mary Lonan Reilly lives in Rochester's Assisi Heights, where she is the archivist for the Sisters of St. Francis community.

James Dean, Eat Your Heart Out
by Steve Swanson

Among the commemorative postage stamps that immortalize celebrities of the past was one that pictured James Dean, our star-crossed mid-century film hero. There he was, forever young and rebellious, twenty identical perforated images of him. The giant we all remembered with his high cheekbones, prominent forehead and tousled brown hair looked out from identical inch by half inch stamps, his pouting lips seeming to say, "You'll never understand me."

With our chopped and channeled cars, our big band and soft rock music, our rolled-up jeans and penny loafers, many of us Midwestern teens thought we wanted to be James Dean back then. We gathered to try to prove that to each other at our local drive-in.

Ken Heacock, a Carleton graduate, our high school chemistry teacher, and my wrestling coach, sensed the need for Northfield teenagers to have a gathering spot. In the spring of 1948, in a marathon of after-school, evening and weekend work sessions, he built, on old Highway 3 South, near where the Family Physicians' Clinic now stands, Heacock's A & W Drive-in.

He hired a few of us to help lay the foundation, mixing cement and laying block. Ken Heacock hammered together most of the building himself. When it was finished, he bought equipment, fenced and gravelled the parking lot, hired cooks, dishwashers and carhops, and opened for his first summer's business.

Heacock's was an instant success. Everyone who worked there went to Northfield High School, as did most of the customers. The building was spartan, but the menu featured all the classic mid-century fare-- hamburgers, fries, onion rings, ice cream and frosty glass mugs foaming over with root beer--all served on those tricky little window trays by smiling, gum-chewing carhops wearing bobby sox and saddle shoes. These foods featured the same addictive salt, sugar and oil that McDonalds later parlayed into a multi-billion dollar bonanza.

At Heacock's we ate, talked, migrated from car to car, and organized impromptu caravans to the Grand Theater or to nearby towns for a movie. We invited each other to car-radio dances on the Carleton tennis courts or challenged each other to climb the new St. Olaf water tower. We tried (not very hard) to keep each other from learning the whereabouts of the weekend slumber parties and campouts.

In those pretty good old days, Ken Heacock helped us grow up. He created a wholesome place for many of us to work and most of us to meet and eat. Some of us may have tried to look like James Dean, but we lacked his rebellious reputation. The only recurring sin on that site was gluttony.

Steve Swanson is an author, English professor at St. Olaf College, and Lutheran clergyman. He lives in Northfield.

Physics Lesson
by Steve Swanson

I earned eighteen college credits in physics and worked two summers in the St. Olaf physics shop. Others in our group took high school and college physics. Obert Tufte later earned his Ph.D. in physics. But one summer night in 1949, in Ames Park, where the Jesse James carnival still sets up, a sideshow barker taught my high school friends and me a lifetime lesson in basic physics.

Behind him in his booth were shelves full of potential prizes--kewpie dolls and teddy bears--and you could also win money. Like the baseball throw, this was a knock-down game, but very much hands-on and far more sophisticated. In carnival lingo, this game is known as the swinger.

A ten-pound steel ball the size of a softball hung on a cable from the canopy, and beneath it, a bowling pin was nudged into a v-shaped slot in the counter. The challenge was to swing the ball toward the rear of the booth, barely miss the narrowest part of the bowling pin, then knock the pin over from behind as the ball swung forward again.

The barker could do it every time. "Look," he demonstrated, leaning toward us, his voice almost as confidential and inviting as Ingrid Bergman's, " It's easy. You just swing the ball past the pin and let it knock down the pin from behind." Swing-knock, swing-knock.

It did look easy--and it was, because when he swung the ball, he set the pin off-center.

One after another we paid our dollars and took turns trying. Each time we tried, the carnie pressed the pin perfectly into the v-notch, exactly under the center point of the suspended ball. Not even God could have hit that pin without changing the immutable and eternal natural laws. Newton's laws of motion and the pendulum effect made that change impossible. If the ball missed the pin by one inch on the forward swing, it would miss it by one inch on the return.

We lost $52 among us.   Rubes we were--small town hicks. Afterward, Paul Sherwin took revenge by backing his oil-guzzling '38 Oldsmobile behind the tent and smothering it in a cloud of blue petroleum smoke.

John Sletten had a better plan of attack.   He unilaterally walked down the street for a chat with city attorney Burt Sawyer, who was already in his jammies.   Burt dressed and called officer Lenno Brandt, and they arrested the barker for illegal gambling.   Swinger is known as a gaffed game or a flat joint.   In other words, it is a scam that is impossible to win. Bail, oh miraculous bail, was set at $52.

Monday morning the six of us had to appear in court.   Judge Silliman gave us a stern lecture on the evil of gambling, then gave us our money back.

I have never gambled since--not a single quarter in a single slot machine, not a single dollar for a single lottery ticket--never.

Point of Departure
by Tom Veblen

The night of my birth was, believe it or not, dark and stormy.

In the late afternoon a sudden blizzard moved in from the north, and by nightfall, as the story goes, when my mother arrived at the hospital ready to give birth, the storm was roaring like a banshee. It was a dark and stormy night.

The Red River Valley is notorious for the ferocity and seeming malevolence of its snow storms. At the time of my birth, before the days of scientific weather forecasting, storms arrived unannounced. Featuring bone-numbing Arctic winds and precipitous temperature drops, they were a force to be reckoned with. In fact, they were killers.

Chatham Corner, three miles south of Hallock on Highway 75, was responsible for a number of blizzard-induced deaths. Chatham Corner is, in fact, two corners situated twelve miles due north of Kennedy. Highway 75 going north takes a ninety degree turn west, runs a quarter of a mile to where the Great Northern Railway's Chatham elevator once stood, and then takes another ninety degree turn north for the three mile straight run on into Hallock. Oddly enough, the railroad just west of the highway proceeds north straight as a string. Why, in the middle of an ancient, featureless, flat-as-a-pancake lake bed would a road paralleling the railroad be given two ninety degree turns? Go figure.

When the highway was built many years after the railroad, the Red River Valley survey had been completed and the land laid out in mile square (360 acre) sections. Because the world is round, squaring off sections of it calls for an adjustment to accommodate its gradually narrowing surface going north. Highway 75's engineers were instructed to position the road along the north-south section lines. They felt compelled, as a consequence, to put a crook in the right of way every ten miles or so. Unconsciously they created a barrier for south blowing snow at Chatham Corner--a car trap for disoriented drivers traversing that treeless prairie during blizzards.

In my youth, hardly a winter went by without someone getting caught in this trap. A fierce snow storm would sweep in from the north. A dog-tired blizzard-disoriented driver, peering intently through fogged windows, would miss one or the other of the Chatham turns and drive his car straight into a snow-filled ditch. Hours later the driver and passengers would be found huddled in the idling car--most times alive, but not so rarely dead, the victims of carbon monoxide poisoning.

The most dramatic scenarios involved night drivers who, in below zero temperature, misgauged the turn, skidded into the snow-filled ditch at Chatham, and tried to walk three miles to Hallock. On crystal nights that typically follow a deep-winter blizzard, the lights of Hallock appeared to be just blocks away. You could almost touch them, it seemed. And so, the impatient driver, lightly clad and facing into a fifteen to twenty mile per hour wind, would give it a shot--likely as not to be found later, short of Hallock, frozen to death by the side of the road.

The day I was born, my father, Edgar Veblen, had business that carried him forty miles south of Hallock to the small town of Argyle, where he was when the storm hit. Prudence dictated that he hole up for the night and return to Hallock after the storm passed, but my impending birth triggered his homing instinct. He phoned my mother before leaving Argyle and told her to expect him home by dinner.

Driving a wind-swept Highway 75 north into the teeth of the storm, through Stephen, Donaldson and Kennedy, he arrived at the Chatham corner without incident. And there his luck ran out. Snow had drifted over the east-west segment of the corner's turn, blocking his way. While attempting to turn around and head back to Kennedy, he slid off the shoulder and, like so many others before him, into the snow-filled ditch. He knew better than to attempt the walk to Hallock or to risk freezing to death in the ditch or risk carbon monoxide poisoning, so he left the car and headed south, with his back to the wind, to find shelter in a farmhouse several miles back.

Amid the birthing, as the storm intensified, my mother became anxious. This was no time for her husband to be out on the open prairie. His arrival home was long overdue, the phone lines were down, and somebody had to go find him. She called on her brother Loe, a rural mail carrier who was fully conscious of the dangers involved. But Loe had a high-clearance, rumble-seated Model T Ford coupe and a buffalo skin coat, so he felt up to the challenge.

Cranking up the Ford, Loe headed south out of Hallock and down Highway 75 to Chatham Corner. There he discovered the snow-blocked stretch of road and my father's abandoned car. No Edgar--but no mystery. Ed had obviously walked the ditch line south, the wind at his back, looking for shelter. Taking to foot, Loe followed in what he presumed was my father's track and soon stumbled into that same farmhouse.

They say that two heads are better than one, and it may be true. But then again, given the ensuing events, there is reason to question this old saw. My father and Loe were determined to make it back to Hallock for the big bang. Their scheme? Walk the ditch line south to Kennedy. Borrow or rent a sled and team of horses, and head back, straight north, for Hallock.

Their scheme failed. Though the intrepid travelers were up for the game, the horses weren't. Driven to the north edge of Kennedy, they faced into the wind-driven snow and refused to brace it. Whipped, they simply took a stand, heads down, shock still. Nor would they take a lead. That ended it for the night. The defeated men turned the horses with the wind and headed back to the barn to bed down in the hay mow, where men and the beasts huddled in the cold and waited out the storm. Meanwhile, back in Hallock, I showed up without the company of father or uncle on the dark and stormy night of December 17, 1929. The storm might serve as an allegory for the difficulty faced by our little town on the prairie; hard times preceded it and hard times followed.

A few months before my birth, the Hallock Bank, where my father worked, went bust. For the next two years, jobless, with his savings gone and his family growing, Edgar Veblen scrambled to make a living, but so did everybody else. His brother's two teenage sons joined us. How he managed is as much a mystery today as it was then. When the Northwestern Mutual Life Insurance Company came looking for someone to oversee their foreclosed farms in Kittson County, they offered $16 a week, and my dad took the job.

My family's predicament was typical.   My grandfather owned and operated one of the town's most successful general stores for forty years.   Seemingly overnight, as gain prices plummeted in the 20's, and his farmer customers went broke, the store turned from an asset to a liability. By 1930 it was losing money and quickly going out of business after customers failed to honor their debts and suppliers withdrew credit.   Over fifteen years, from the early 20's to the late 30's, Grandfather's wealth disappeared.

Downtown Hallock, photo courtesy of Kittson County Historical Society

The place where we lived, Hallock, was nicely sited on a wooded bend of the Two Rivers, but a long way from any place worth getting to-- ten miles east of the Red River, 365 miles north of Minneapolis, and 75 gravelly, pot-holed miles south of Winnipeg.   It was a Lake Wobegone kind of place.   The men really were strong (farming will do that for you), the women really were good looking (where better than among the Nordics to look for clean-limbed, fair-complexioned beauties who bloom both early and late), and the children were, in their parents' aspirations at least, all above average.

Charles Hallock, journalist and avid hunter, and James J. Hill, founder of the Great Northern Railway, were the unwitting collaborators who brought this town to life.   Hill immigrated to the United States from Canada in 1856, settled in St. Paul, and became enamored with the freight business.   He looked over the Great American Desert and imagined a rural paradise replacing the endless expanse of grass, buffalo and Indians. By the 1870's his dream evolved into the creation of a transcontinental railroad that went north from the Twin Cities across the lake and prairie country of central Minnesota to the Red River and from there to the Rocky Mountains and on to the Pacific.

Hill's grand vision was to populate the prairie with sturdy farmers and enterprising merchants, all to be served by his Great Northern Railway. He would recruit hale, God-fearing, northern European yeomen to populate the prairie. They would farm the land, raise rich crops, and send their produce to market over his rails. Towns would grow and prosper, along with the railroad. It would be a prosperous and self-fulfilling empire, a peaceful kingdom in the bowels of a mighty democratic republic.

Charles Hallock, publisher of *Forest and Stream* magazine, discovered the Red River Valley of Hill's inland empire before other Americans. He was entranced by the area's abundant wildlife that included buffalo, elk, bear, wolf, antelope, geese, ducks and grouse. Bent on providing his Eastern readers access to this sportsman's paradise, he bought land along the north branch of the Two Rivers, and put up a hunting lodge, the Hallock Hotel. His idea clicked, and hunters poured in from Eastern cities and from Europe.

Hill sent in surveyors, engineers, and land speculators to plat the land and charter and organize towns. In the next forty years, thanks to Hill's railroad and a growing demand for wheat, Charles Hallock's hunting lodge grew to a bustling market center with a population of 2000. The economic and political hub of Kittson County, Hallock boasted two grain elevators, the county court house, a weekly newspaper, (The *Kittson County Enterprise*) a post office, and a full complement of general stores, banks, land offices, blacksmiths and saloons. Hallock, a town secured by an enterprising business community, was a model for the myriad prairie towns created further to the west and north.

It was too good to last. By the time my classmates and I were born in 1929 and into the early 1930's, Hill's vision had fallen apart. Minnesota's prairie-bound small towns, once vital centers of commerce and culture and governance, magnets for the speculative, the industrious and the enterprising, had become casualties of a decade-long drought and a national depression. What we were too young to know is that our parents and grandparents and their peers, having earlier succeeded far beyond their wildest expectations, found themselves suddenly impoverished by forces beyond their control.

After a decade of declining grain and farm land prices, there wasn't a sound business left. Those that had somehow escaped bankruptcy were now teetering on its brink. The community was virtually cashless--its economy reduced to mostly barter and subsistence. People who could leave had left for cities to the south and east, or if they were adventurous, to California. The population dropped to 1200. Those not able or motivated to leave mostly just toughed it out. By the mid 1930's, pummeled by collapsed markets for farm products, Hallock had gone from a place of opportunity to a place people came from--a point of departure.

By the time I arrived on the scene, forty years or so after Hallock's founding, most of the pioneers were gone, but their stories were very much alive. Their sons and daughters, the adults in my early life, lived frugally and modestly through the Great Depression and experienced first hand the requirements of enterprise. They absorbed and understood the principle, and by example and admonition, they passed the message along. Work hard, work smart, think hard and never take an unconsidered risk.

But hard work and hard thinking weren't enough. Initiative counted too. We learned to press on. Someone willing and able to undertake money-making projects on his own like raising chickens in the back yard, catching and selling pollywogs after school, or finding a part-time job gained peer and community respect. By the time we were 15, encouraged to make our own way and hold up our end of a bargain, we thought of ourselves as adults.

As students we were expected to go seriously about our studies, and we accepted the authority of our teachers. Period. And when our teachers coached extracurricular activities and sports, they assumed we would participate wholeheartedly and enthusiastically. And we did. Many of our older siblings and friends spent summers at CCC camps, a youth version of the WPA, where, in addition to other public works, they built walkways, retaining walls and control dams at state parks such as Lake Bronson and Itasca.

Looking back, it is obvious that we were poor, but we didn't feel underprivileged because we had supportive parents, teachers, and adults who never let on. I thought the hoboes who sometimes came knocking at our door represented the way things were supposed to be. My mother greeted them pleasantly, set them to some task around the yard, and gave them a good meal, which they would eat on the back step with my sister and me intently observing the whole process. We came to know that times were tough--and that if we didn't pay attention, we could wind up just as they were--down and out.

My high school class graduated in 1947. It's hard to imagine a less pretentious or more equalitarian Minnesota nice gaggle of young people. We were the very model of a classic rural American group-- fifteen boys and sixteen girls, most of whom had been together since kindergarten--a mix of farm and town kids, mostly Norwegian, mostly blue-eyed and blond, who mostly spoke English with Norwegian accents. The two notable exceptions were Norma Olsenowski, a tall, raw-boned Polish girl who morphed into our class valedictorian, and Jim Carrigan, a darkly handsome Irish kid, who became our salutatorian and went on, no surprise to the rest of us, to a distinguished academic and legal career.

I realize now that we were a very privileged group of young people because our parents and our teachers, whether at home, in school, or on our jobs, equipped us for an escape from the diminishing economic opportunities out there on the northern prairie. A handful of class members stayed on in Hallock to find fulfillment, but for most of us the future lay down Highway 75, around the Chatham Corner and south, the wind at our backs, out into the wider world.

We traveled to our final destinations as teachers or business practitioners or lawyers or airline pilots or whatever, not as victims or woebegone pilgrims, but as enterprisers, fully prepared to elect, for the rest of lives, our own points of departure.

Tom Veblen, a retired general management consult, lives in Washington, D.C. His special interest in the role of business in society led to a recently published work, "The Way of Business: An Inquiry into Meaning and Superiority."

Red River Valley Sugar Beet Harvest
by Tom C. Veblen

My yearly visits to Hallock don't usually have unintended consequences. Survey the crops, talk with farmers, bankers, and local businessmen, pay some bills, drink some coffee, and eat some good Scandinavian cookies. Depart with a reassurance that American values are still safe in at least one corner of the country.

The summer of 1995 was different. A casual conversation with John and Jeff Deere turned to sugar beets, an increasingly important aspect of their farming operation. The Deere brothers were having trouble finding truck drivers for the upcoming harvest, and despite their best recruiting efforts, were still one driver short. "Well," said I, somewhat to the surprise of all, "if you really can't find someone, let me know."

Their call came in mid-September, so on September 28, my natural aversion to labor offset by nostalgia and curiosity, I headed west.

Occasionally I do feel nostalgia for Hallock and my boyhood there. How could it be otherwise? Boy Scouts....canoeing trips..fishing and hunting...high school...hockey...chorus....pals and dates. Softened by the passage of a half century, even the drudgery of summer work stirs emotion. House painting... telephone line work... digging ditches... mowing lawns... farm work during planting and harvesting seasons...tractor driving... grain swathing... combining... grain shoveling... plowing...truck driving. Fourteen hour days....mile long furrows.... mosquitoes.... heat.... wind..... dust...sweat... Though viewed at the time as gut-wrenching, the work now elicits mostly thoughts about outcomes: muscles hardened, skills acquired, pride and money in the bank. Mostly it was the kind of work that made enrolling in college look like a sensible thing to do.

Weather permitting, the Red River Valley's sugar beet harvest gets underway the first days of October and lasts three or more weeks, depending on the weather. Temperatures over 55 and under 30 produce beets unsuitable for storage. Too much rain, sleet or hail causes machinery to bog down in the mud. If there is snow or excessive wind, the harvest comes to a halt, and disgruntled harvesters head for the machine shop, Margie's cafe, or home to wait for the first chance to get back to work.

I arrived ready for work on September 30, and learned that the beets were too warm. Since the harvest hadn't begun, this would be defined as a delay rather than an interruption, but the effect was the same. Frustration at not being able to start was probably even more intense than that caused by having work suspended by circumstance. Then, wouldn't you know, the temperature dropped, and the wind started to blow, and a light mist turned to rain.

After a week's delay, the sky cleared, and a drying wind began its work. We slid into Deere's soggy beet field, and the harvest began. Harvesting beets is a simple piece of work, but not, by any account, is it easy. To prepare beets for harvest, it is necessary to cut off their tops with a rotobeater, a tractor-pulled piece of machinery, the axles of which cause knife-like blades to whir through beet tops at high speed. After the beets are topped, they are lifted out of the ground by a lifter that is pulled by a tractor whose eight offset digging wheels, embedded in the ground on either side of four beet rows, spew beets onto a conveyor and into a truck.

When the ground is dry and the soil crumbly, beets are easily parted from the surrounding dirt, and harvesting proceeds with little or no fuss. Wet soil causes problems. As Deere lowered the digger's wheels into the soggy ground and we started forward, it was evident that extracting beets from wet ground is not a task for the faint of heart nor the mechanically disinclined. The next twenty-four hours was a reeducation in the vicissitudes of farming.

When wet, Kittson County soil, referred to by natives as gumbo, is a malevolent force of prodigious dimensions. Once disturbed, it turns from axle grease to library paste to glue, whereupon it clings with unrelenting tenacity to any exposed surface: tires, axles, running boards, tractor and truck floors, boots, gloves, clothing, thermos bottles, eye glasses--you name it. As it builds layers, it corrupts machinery. Building in the crannies of trucks and tractors, it forces panels to part and hydraulic controls to break down. Setting around truck and tractor lights, it dislodges lenses and shorts electrical leads. Clogging the lifter's wheels, it forces them to the surface.

Cleaning gumbo from a lifter's digging wheels is a character-building exercise. Once plastered to a piece of equipment, with its surface water squeezed out, gumbo becomes plastic. In such a state it resists all but the most determined efforts to separate it from the metal to which it clings. The weapon of choice in this war is a hoe fashioned from a four-foot steel rod. Presumably its sharpened end, plunged deeply into the gumbo, permits one to lift mud from metal in great gobs and with great efficiency. This theory is mostly a delusion.

Plunging the hoe into plasticized gumbo turns out to be a mistake because the force of such an effort causes the metal rod to spring back, turning it into a deadly weapon that indiscriminately strikes the wielder, innocent bystanders, and vulnerable parts of the equipment. On such occasion, with shins bruised and knuckles skinned, the hoe wielder's thoughts turn to murder or self immolation. To experience this in the dead of night, under the glare of tractor and lifter lights, with a raw wind whistling out of the north and two wise-ass, kibitzing truck drivers standing by is to learn rage anew. Professional gumbo scrapers have learned a few tricks that maximize effort while minimizing frustration.

Beet harvesting in the Red River Valley is a suspenseful kind of game with its own unique object, rules, and competitive dynamics. The valley's weather is unforgiving, and memories of failed harvests cause a certain kind of obsessive behavior in the campaign's participants as they try to beat the clock in the thirty days or so between beet maturity and first snow. During that window of opportunity, the game players, organized into teams of field equipment operators and truck drivers, must dig and deliver more than eight million tons of beets in a timely and cost-effective manner or see them destroyed as the valley temperature drops and ruins the crop.

The rules of the game relate to the overall task and to the actions that make for effective team play. Beets can only be harvested when their internal temperature lies between 30 and 40 degrees Fahrenheit. Their tops must be cut, and they must be harvested during specified hours, depending on the producer's allotment and distance from the piler. Truck drivers are expected to drive safely, observe the law, yield when meeting a loaded truck, ignore wildlife when loaded, and not cut corners when loaded. They must observe the piler's yard rules, yield to outgoing trucks, stop before entering the scale, keep their place in line, follow dump instructions and be civil. The team rules, though unstated, assume the application of common sense: come to work well rested and ready to work, stay alert, deliver on your promises, try to make things work right, and put your back into it when necessary.

Once into it, the mystique of harvest is easy to understand. It must succeed if the entire enterprise is to succeed. It is the culmination of the full year's work for the producer who owns the entire enterprise. It is an all-American, go-for-broke kind of activity that's complex and intense enough to challenge the passions, intellect, and culture of those involved.

While there's a lot to say about sugar beets as a social phenomenon, nothing in the whole chain of enterprise so captures the attention of its participants as the activities involved in harvesting the beets themselves. Referred to as a campaign, beet harvest absorbs the whole community for its brief duration.

Once underway, the Deere team operated around the clock in twelve-hour shifts starting at noon. The fundamental challenge, given the beating that equipment and men take under a twenty-four hour regimen in the open fields, is to keep men, tractors, harvest machines and trucks in sync and running. Avoidance of downtime becomes an obsession.

Fortunately the Deere brothers were totally committed to getting things done right and right now. We went into the harvest with all systems go. The Deere team was fairly typical of teams throughout the valley. Three professional farmers provided management, operated the lifter and rotobeater, and maintained the equipment. Five truck drivers, a college student, a neighbor who took time off from the bus plant in Pembina, a 40-year-old off-season chemical spray pilot, the president of the Hallock bank, and I transported beets from lifter to piler and generally lent a hand as circumstances dictated.

The harvest rolled right along, except for two nights when the temperature dropped below freezing. Two and a half weeks of dry weather saw all the valley beets harvested. Generally, throughout the valley, both tonnage and sugar content were good. Locally, there were no serious accidents. Though our team experienced the normal interruptions associated with mechanical contrivances, our failures were minor and readily repairable. Nobody drove into the ditch, tore up a transmission or hit anything like the deer that bounded out of ditches onto the road at twilight. Given the proximity to whirring shafts and the wear and tear of twelve hour days, farming is a notoriously dangerous occupation, but we were careful and lucky.

And so it ended. Revitalized, with my nostalgia allayed and my idle curiosity satisfied, I headed for my home in Washington, D.C. fully prepared to reengage in the fight for urban survival. There's something to be said for unintended consequences. It was good to spend time in Hallock, reflecting on change while challenged by the demands of sensible work that needed doing. What a pleasure to find that vocation is still a powerful force in the lives of the people I grew up with, that nature still sets the valley's pace, and that even modest adventure invigorates the soul.

Sugar beet harvest in Kittson County: tractor, lifter, and truck.

Photo courtesy of the Kittson County Enterprise and Marcy Johnson.

Enok School in Kittson County
by Vernon Johnson

Three institutions helped build and shape character and provide stability in our lives. Those institutions were the home, church, and school. Jupiter Township of Kittson County had four country schools and four churches. Now it has one school building that is used as the Town Hall and one vacant church, the East Emmaus Church, that stands as a reminder of the past.

I attended the Enok School--or District #14 South. The Lindquist School, the Bjornberg School, and the Dreher School were located in different areas of the township so that the students who attended did not have to walk too great a distance--maybe two or two and a half miles at the most.

The Enok School was a one-room building with a big wood stove heater in the corner that had a metal jacket around it. In the wintertime, those who sat close to the stove were too hot, and those further away were too cold. The school had a horse barn that was used for a wood shed and two outhouses, one for the boys and one for the girls. We tried to use them while we were outside playing at noon or during our 15 minute recess, but occasionally nature called while we were in school. We would raise our hand to ask permission to make that trip to the relief station. When the weather was nice, we would take our time, but in winter we'd make that trip as quickly as possible.

Fifteen or sixteen families were involved in Enok School. Our house was a mile away, not a bad walk in nice weather. Our dad, Conrad Johnson was very good about giving us a ride with his horse and wagon or horse and sleigh whenever the weather was cold or wet. On our way, we would pick up other kids.

I spent eight years at Enok School, and I still remember my first day. I was playing outside before the bell rang in the morning, and I got thirsty. I went into the building to get a drink of water from the fountain in the corner. Ordinarily the way the fountain worked was that you pushed a button that released the water to bubble and the surplus ran into a pail.

But the pail was not there that day, so water ran onto the floor. Boy, was I scared! I thought I would be punished so I ran outside. As I ran, I peeked at my teacher. She just smiled so I knew things would be okay.

Marjorie Sylvester Ash was my teacher for the first three grades. Edith Bengston was my next teacher. She had the longest tenure at Enok School and was my teacher for five years. I have many fond memories of that time in my life.

One time we took a field trip on a fall Friday afternoon. We literally went to a field across the road from the school. When we came back we were supposed to tell what we had seen. Many reported seeing flowers and birds. One little first grade boy reported that he had seen a lion, and the whole school erupted in laughter. Edith Bengston did not want to laugh at the boy so she turned around and faced the board while her shoulders shook up and down.

I remember the sports we played at school. If we'd get a January thaw, the snow in the field would turn to water and then freeze when the temperature dropped again, providing us with a hockey rink. We'd find a willow branch with a nice curve in the end to use as a hockey stick, and for a puck we'd use frozen horse turds. After two or three whacks, they would be history, but there was always a ready supply nearby with all the horse teams in that area. We had some highly contested hockey games.

Kitten ball was another sport that we enjoyed. A kitten ball was larger than a baseball and not so hard. We were not allowed to use a glove. In spring we would have a play day with neighboring schools. Winners would go to Hallock, where we competed with other country school winners. Axel Johnson gave us a ride in his 1930 one-ton Chevy truck, which added another dimension to the adventure one year. We not only competed in kitten ball, but also in broad jump and relay races. We took top honors in kitten ball.

We had extracurricular activities besides sports, and one of my favorites was declamation. Declamation events gave kids good experience in public speaking. I always had a humorous piece to memorize for competitions with nearby schools. Winners would go to Hallock for county competition. I went to Hallock twice but never won first place there.

Edith Bengston would put on programs once a year for parents and the public. Sometimes it would be at Thanksgiving and sometimes at Christmas. Preparation took about three weeks, which was okay with us because we could spend less time studying and more time practicing for the program. Audience members who filled the school to the brim enjoyed these programs because they got to see and hear what the kids could do.

If the program was held at Christmas, the final highlight came when we exchanged gifts with the kids whose names we had drawn. After that, Santa Claus would come in and give a candy cane to each child. Lunch and games followed the program.

The American Legion gave one eighth grade graduate a trip to Winnipeg each spring. My neighbor pal Gunner Paulson and I were the only two in our class all eight years, so Edith Bengston thought we should both have that trip. Axel Johnson, a Legion member, drove us, and we visited Assinaboine Park and the Parliament Building.

Enok School reunion, 1980

In 1980 we had an all school Enok reunion that was very well attended with former students coming from near and far. We started the reunion in the Enok School building, where we took pictures and visited.

Then we moved to Lake Bronson, where we had rented the school gym. My biggest surprise was meeting Marjorie Sylvester Ash, my first teacher whom I hadn't seen since I was in third grade. We shared a picnic lunch followed by an afternoon of sharing memories of the old school days, and everyone had a wonderful time. As of this writing, the oldest Enok alumna is Nannie Swanson Johnson, age 102.

I look back upon those years before hot lunches, indoor plumbing, and electricity. We carried our little tin lunch pails. Talk about frozen foods! If the food wasn't frozen, at least it was chilled all winter. The bigger kids carried water from the Richard Erlandson farm, a trip that someone had to make every day of the school year. We started with full pails, but by the time we got to school, those buckets were half empty.

The country schools of Jupiter township were too good to be torn down so they took on new lives when they were closed. One was moved to Halma, where it still exists as a house. One was moved to Karlstad, where it is used as the Gospel Tabernacle Church. I don't know what happened to the Dreher School, but Enok school is now used as a Town Hall.

I think of those early days when the teacher had all eight grades in one room and had to keep the attention of each class. I know our teacher had to arrive early to make fires and warm the school before her students showed up. She also was the janitor who had to clean and sweep after school each day. The one room school was a great place to learn the 3 R's and to form friendships. I salute the school and those teachers, and I have great memories and respect for both.

Vernon Johnson and his wife Muriel have lived for 56 years in Lake Bronson on a farm his grandfather homesteaded in 1882. He is a retired farmer and insurance agent.

Julotta 1930
by Vernon Johnson

One tradition that our Swedish forefathers brought to this country was to have a 6 a.m. Christmas morning service called Julotta. When I was 10 years old in 1930, my father, Conrad Johnson, my sister Adeline and I decided that we should get up early and walk to the Julotta at the East Emmaus Lutheran Church. This was not our regular church but one we attended on special occasions, and this was a special occasion.

It was a beautiful, clear, moonlight Christmas morning and not too cold. We dressed warm and walked across the fields over hard packed snow-- a distance of about one mile as the crow flies. If we had walked the road, it would have been a half mile farther. We left for church about 5:15 so that we wouldn't arrive at the last minute. When we got there, quite a few members were already at the church with their sleighs and horses with bells on. The horses were put in the horse barn, which was also on the church grounds. They stayed in the barn so that they would be warm and rested for the trip back home.

Pastor B. N. Glim, who lived in Kennedy, drove his car as far as the Enok store. Somebody from the church met him with horses and sleigh to complete the trip to the church-- another two or three miles.

The church was beautifully decorated. Christmas carols and the sermon were in Swedish. One of the carols was "Var Halsad Skona Morgonstund" which means "All Hail to Thee, O Blessed Morn." The service lasted about an hour. After exchanging greetings with others, it was time to go home. Albert Erlandson and his family lived about four and a half miles northwest of the church, and since they had to drive by our house, they gave us a lift home in their sleigh.

We appreciated the ride, and when we got home daylight was breaking. It was time to do the morning chores, followed by breakfast. The East Emmaus church still stands in the same church yard in Jupiter Township in the southwest corner of section 21 as a memory to the past. I don't think you can find any church in Kittson County that has a 6 a.m. Julotta on Christmas because the East Emmaus Church closed in 1964.

Rural Schools Past
by Bernice Lanik

My elementary school education was acquired in two vastly different rural schools. During the school years from grade one through grade five, I attended Homer school and stayed with my grandparents who lived a block away from the school.

Those five years spent with my grandparents were good years. I had just one teacher during all that time, and in my mind she was a wonderful teacher. She had some help, however. Student teachers supervised by Rural Education came from Winona Normal School, now Winona State University, to practice teach.

The school, a brick building, is still standing, but it serves as the town hall. All eight grades were taught in one large room. Boys and girls had separate cloak rooms. Under the school was a full basement with a furnace and an area for after- school activities and for hot lunch. Mothers came each day to prepare the hot meal.

Although we had electricity, we had no indoor plumbing. We got water from a well behind the building and used the two outhouses in the back yard. It was a super rural school.

Going to school was a joy. I was well-behaved, though too quiet and very shy. I loved to draw and to read the many books the supervisors from the college brought.

A sand box stood in the corner of the room. When we studied different countries of the world, we constructed representations of the areas and their inhabitants. Grandma helped me make costumes for many dolls that we used for natives of many lands.

On May Day, we danced around the May pole. One year my sister, who was two years younger than I, was chosen to be May Queen. Mother made her a red dotted Swiss dress, and Grandma made a blue dotted Swiss for me. My sister's was prettier than mine, I thought, because it had ruffles. Mine was plainer with a gathered skirt. Perhaps I was envious of my younger sister with her ruffles because she was May Queen, but I remember that the whole experience was exciting.

When my brother reached school age, we girls switched schools because we no longer stayed in Homer with my grandparents. The three of us walked a mile and a half to the Martin school in our district. When there was snow, we used skis.

The teacher that first year had a name some of the older children changed to Miss Woodchuck--behind her back, of course. Several students were not much younger than she was. At that time and until rural schools closed, students took a state board examination in the spring of eighth grade. If they did not pass, they attended school until age sixteen.

Martin school students were at a disadvantage. Teachers were young and inexperienced, and we missed the support and help Winona Normal School practice teachers and their supervisors brought into the other school. We shared many texts, rather than having individual copies, and there were few library books. I really missed all the reading materials we had at Homer School. Thank goodness I was an avid reader before I came to this school. One subject we really did learn though was arithmetic--at least I did. Perfect Palmer Method penmanship was also stressed, and many of my generation still practice it.

Since there was no well, older students took turns carrying water in pails from a neighboring farmhouse. We poured it into a water fountain, and each child kept his own folding cup in our desks. Really sanitary!

Our Christmas program was fun. Parents and friends expected and got a real production. Practice started shortly after Thanksgiving. We practiced plays and memorized poems and songs. Sheets were fastened to wires stretched across a front section of the room for curtains, and the curtains were opened and closed for the various acts. Since this was such a big social event, the whole neighborhood showed up.

The candle-lit tree (yes, because there was no electricity) was surrounded by gifts and boxes of candy. Students drew names and bought a gift for the person whose name they had drawn. Santa passed out gifts, and everyone had a wonderful time.

Another big social event was the end of the year school picnic. We played games, ran races, and received awards for attendance. The food was wonderful, as was the idea that we would have no school for the next three months!

After my first year, Martin School had a hard time hanging onto teachers. One year there were three different teachers. Martin School lost the first teacher after Christmas because she could not find a nearby boarding place and had to walk to and from Witoka--four miles each way. The year I graduated we had two different teachers. One I related to very well was 17 years old and had just finished her teacher training. She came in the spring and finished out the year.

Rural schools are an important part of our heritage. Farm children got the basics of education needed for rural life or for taking their first step into the world beyond. Many continued their education at colleges and universities and did very well. Relatives and neighbors joined in events of student life in a way that we don't see in today's larger schools.

Homer School in the early 1900's

Bernice Lanik, a retired fifth grade teacher, lives in Winona. She and her husband Charles have four children, ten grandchildren, and four great grandchildren. She enjoys sewing, reading, and doll collecting.

A Cordial Calamity
by Frances J. Arenz

In 1967 we were living on Howard Street in Winona, but we were in the process of building a new home on Lake Boulevard. Ralph Stender from Stender Cabinets came to our house to consult with us about designs for our kitchen cabinets.

He spread out blueprints on the dining room table. "Let's see now," Ralph said, "I have this empty space above the refrigerator. Would you like to leave that as a wall area for hanging a picture, or should I put a small door there? You could use it for a safe."

My husband Bernie studied the blueprint for a moment or two before making his decision. "I'd like that space for a liquor cabinet if that's okay with you," he said as he turned to me.

"Oh sure. That's okay," I replied. We didn't have liquor in our house when I was a kid, and I'm not a drinker, but I figured it would be fine for Bernie to have a liquor cabinet.

We moved into our new home on Easter Sunday. A few weeks later we made a special trip across the river to The Wine House at Bluff Siding. We spent a lot of time and money choosing various cordials, brandies and wines to stock the bare cupboard above the refrigerator.

Once in a while Bernie would bring a shoe salesman home, and once in a while friends and relatives would stop by. It was only when visitors arrived that we would use the liquor cabinet. My husband would ask if they would like a snifter of brandy or a finger of Scotch. He served each drink with ceremony and aplomb that he hadn't possessed in our old home. It was a nice thing to do, and I liked having a liquor cabinet.

A couple of years later, I noticed that the cabinet wood was becoming dull and dry, so I took a small step ladder from the garage and found some lemon oil under the sink. With a large wad of cheesecloth clutched in my hand, I climbed the ladder and started to oil the cabinets. I started at the top where the cupboards began and worked my way over to the liquor cabinet door.

When I opened the door, I noticed that the lovely bottles were all still there, but some contained just a small amount of liquid. Other bottles had no more than a trace. "What an unkempt, messy way of doing things," I thought.

I took all the bottles out of the cabinet and set them on the kitchen table. I chose two of the most decorative bottles, and using a funnel began the task of pouring all the dark-colored liquids into one bottle and all the light-colored ones into the other bottle. I carried all the empties out to the trash.

I don't know how long it was after I completed this project when my husband brought Harvey Blick home with him. Harvey was the athletic shoe salesman who called on the Arenz Shoe Store.

It was customary in those days for the vendor to take the owner of the store out to dinner in appreciation of the order he had received. Most often the dinner would be at the Hot Fish Shop, which was located close to our house on Lake Boulevard. It was easy for Bernie to stop off at our house first for a before-dinner drink and to show off his new house and liquor cabinet.

"Well Harvey, would you like a finger of Scotch?"

"That I would. That I would," answered Harvey.

I sat in the parlor with Harvey, who admired our lake view while Bernie retreated to the kitchen. I remembered how I had cleaned up the liquor cabinet and hoped my husband would be impressed with my organizational talent.

Instead of the delighted wonder-of-it-all and compliments that I expected, I heard expletives bouncing off the walls in the kitchen, accompanied by exclamations of "Where in the world is the Scotch?" A brief silence followed, then a realization, no doubt that just maybe.... and well, I guess so.....followed by several "Oh no's." There stood my husband, framed in the archway leading from the parlor to the kitchen, with a bottle in each hand. He was waving them frantically over his head and asking, "What's going on here?"

I explained the logic of my neatness. I had made a creative decision to separate the dark from the light. Was I expected to know that so and so did not mix well with such and such?

There ensued a rapid explanation about Canadian Club not mixing with Rhine Castle, vermouth and tequila were not at all compatible, and how whiskey and brandy combined with Scotch could be a disaster. The guys talked about how kids at barn dances used to get sick after gathering up and combining the remains from everyone's drinks. Bernie once got so sick from doing this that his mother took him to the doctor. Not until my husband dumped out both bottles and poured out two glasses of lager for the men and a glass of soda for me did the whole calamity come to an end.

We moved from Lake Boulevard twenty years later. Our present ranch-style house sits on an acre of land. We have a walk-in pantry that I naturally have easy access to. Three deep shelves of exotic potent potables line the wall to the left. Most of these bottles were Christmas, birthday or some other holiday gifts.

We don't entertain shoe salesmen anymore because the Arenz Shoe Store closed after my husband's retirement. The pretty bottles stay quietly resting, although once in a while I notice that one of them is dying on the shelf. I then uncork it and replenish any other bottle that will hold its contents. Thus, there has never been a real closing to the calamitous event. It seems like an unfinished story. You might say that some people never learn their lesson.

Frances Arenz was born in South Dakota and attended Mt. St. Claire College in Clinton, Iowa. She met her husband in Sioux City, and they moved to Winona in 1949, where they raised three children. She enjoys writing, traveling and visiting with her two grandchildren.

Taxi
by Tom Kropidlowski

Once upon a time when I was a young man, I worked part-time as a cab driver, an experience that I will remember all my life. I could write a book about my life as a cab driver, but I will settle for writing about some of my most memorable disasters.

I worked mainly at night, so I picked up a lot of drunks, hookers, and welfare people. It is ironic that people on welfare who could not afford a car were the ones using cabs the most. Some of them were very nice folks, but others were very annoying. When the annoying ones got their checks, they would buy a dozen loaves of bread and a few other groceries and tell the cab driver to deliver the food to the housing projects so the kids could help unload them. Then they would have the cab driver drop them off at one of the downtown bars.

The first time I drove cab I had to learn how to use the radio and learn all the streets and house number systems in town. My friend was in the passenger seat when I stopped at the depot to pick up a guy and his wife. They had just come from Rochester, where the man had undergone back surgery. I put him and his wife in the back seat, and as I drove, I tried to avoid hitting too many bumps because he was still in pain.

I owned a Plymouth with power brakes that only had to be touched to bring the car to a gentle stop, but the cabs were Fords with brakes that needed work. The driver had to push the pedal down to the floor before anything happened. A situation demanded that I make a quick stop, and I jammed on the brakes so hard that the passenger and his wife slid off the seat. I looked in back and saw them holding on to the front seat and trying to get up from the floor and regain their composure. My friend just held his head and shook it from side to side. I apologized to the couple and hoped I hadn't delivered a medical set-back to the poor guy.

The drunks, on average, were pretty good tippers. I would take them to a bar, and they would tell me to pick them up at a certain time. One old guy was about 75 or 80 years old, and nobody wanted to haul him. He smelled bad but always had money for his fare. On my first encounter with him, I picked him up at the Williams Hotel and Bar and took him to the Legion Club. He was pretty well saturated, and on the way to the Legion he threw up in my cab. After I dropped him off, I went back to the cab stand, where I was met by several laughing drivers who knew this guy. I told them I refused to drive that cab until they cleaned it out.

Another misadventure came after I picked up a nurse at the old hospital one night at 11 p.m. Shorty, one of the cab company owners, usually drove her because she was one of his best customers. He asked me to pick her up one night because he was too busy, and he added that I should "handle her with kid gloves." I said that this would be no problem.

I picked her up and took her to her apartment. When I walked around the cab to open the front door for her, she asked me to turn on the light so she would not fall. Cab dome lights are always shut off because many customers do not like to enable neighbors and passers-by to see them coming and going, I had to open the back door on her side to switch on the dome light. While I was performing this maneuver, she got ready to exit the cab by putting one hand on the dashboard and the other on the post that separates the front and back door.

I didn't notice her hand when I slammed the back door shut. When she let out a scream that you could hear a block away, I noticed that I had slammed her hand in the door. After apologizing profusely, I went back to the cab stand where Shorty was nervously smoking cigarette after cigarette. When he asked me how it had gone, I replied, "Piece of cake." When I told him what really happened, he almost swallowed his cigarette. After he calmed down, I assured him that I thought she was okay.

He smoked a half pack of cigarettes while repeating, " She's going to sue us. I know she is going to sue us." She never did sue us, even though she had a reputation for being a difficult person. I guess I got lucky. However, because of this unpleasant incident, I was never sent to drive her anywhere again. I got lucky several times. No babies were ever born in my cab, and I didn't have any major accidents. After a couple of years, I retired from cab driving and moved on to other careers.

Tom Kropidlowski grew up in Winona's east end. He worked as a cab driver, a reserve police officer, a furniture factory worker and carpenter. He is retired and living in Pickwick. He has two adult children.

Driver's Training
by Eleanor Davidson

My twin brothers Ronald and Donald were not old enough to drive dad's 1930 plush Chevy 4-door with a big trunk on the back, but like most boys, they were mighty interested in cars. Dad kept his car in the garage at our place near Lanesboro, and like many people in the late 30's, he kept his keys in the ignition. This provided a temptation that the boys were unable to resist.

One day Ronald went to the garage and slid open the big door and also opened the small side door. He started the car and raced the engine. Nothing happened, and he shut off the engine and came out and closed all the doors. No harm was done, and Ronald had won some bragging rights.

When Donald heard about his brother's adventure, he decided to try his hand at starting the Chevy, but he was not quite as careful. He entered the small side garage door without opening the big sliding door, and he entered the passenger side of the car and didn't shut the door. He slid over into the driver's seat, turned the key, started the motor, and put the car into reverse.

Suddenly we heard a crash, and we ran to look. Donald had backed the Chevy out of the garage without opening the door. The weight of the car had pushed the garage door open and knocked it off its tracks, so the door landed on top of the car.

Lucky for Donald, the big steel box trunk and spare tire on the back of the Chevy shielded the back end of the car from the impact. But because he had forgotten to close the car's passenger door, that door was nearly ripped off its hinges. The coach work in those old Chevies was made of wood, and the passenger door hung from that post like a broken twig.

Donald cried and repaired the garage door and fixed the car door as best he could. Despite its damaged hinge, the door closed neatly. We had friends visiting us, and we kids convinced Mom not to tell Dad about the car door.

Mom never said a word, but she really should have. Every Wednesday and Saturday night we went to Lanesboro to do our shopping and socializing. My brothers always sat in the front with Dad, while Mom and I sat in the back. Ron and Don always hurried to get in while Dad was still in the house, and they always entered the car through the driver's side so they wouldn't have to open the passenger door.

One day later that summer my dad decided to check the battery before we started out. The battery was on the passenger side. When Dad opened the door, it nearly dropped to the ground. I think he swore in Norwegian because I didn't understand a word. He couldn't imagine what had happened to the door. The boys and Mom felt so guilty that they confessed to the truth and the cover-up. Although my dad was angry, he didn't punish the boys.

Both boys eventually became excellent drivers, and Donald drove cars for an auto dealership. Years later the family, including my dad, laughed as they retold this story at family get-togethers, but everyone used it as an example of why keys should never be left in the ignition.

Donald Davidson

Eleanor Davidson was born near Mable and grew up near Lanesboro. She moved to Rushford in 1971. She has three adult sons and one adult daughter, and she works at the Rushford Historical Society Depot Museum

The Old Raincoat
by Florence Edwardson

There are some things in life I am thankful for and others that I would have rather done without. In that latter group I would like to include an old raincoat I had when I was a kid. Although it kept me dry and warm, I hated it with all my heart, soul and mind. It was an irritation every rainy day and every day when it looked like it might rain.

I'll never forget the day I made my first acquaintance with that coat. My pa came home from town with a bundle in his hands and remarked, "I have something for you to keep you warm and dry when you walk to school and back. Let's try it on." He unwrapped the package and draped a raincoat around me.

After seeing it, I wished the floor would open up and swallow me and the coat. It was the most horrid black thing. A scarecrow would have refused to wear it. But guess who did wear it? You guessed. Little old me. At first I thought I'd get out of wearing it because it was way too big for me. Two people my size could swim in it. Pa smiled and explained that it had to be a little big so that I'd grow into it. I never did grow that much. Not only was it big, but it also was second-hand, sporting several big patches. When I put things in one of the two large pockets, I'd have to reach nearly to the ground to retrieve them.

When I finally worked up the nerve to ask Pa where he had gotten the thing, he told me that he had picked it up at one of the local clothing stores. Holy Cow, the proprietor must have been tickled pink when he got rid of that old relic. Maybe it had been Noah's raincoat.

I'm sure I wished many times that it would not rain on a school day, but of course it did, and I had to trudge along in that gosh awful thing. I had a hard time walking because it was so long I kept tripping on it. I had to hitch it up with one hand and carry my dinner pail in the other. The funny thing was that nobody made fun of me. That in itself was humiliating. It was bad enough having to wear that coat on rainy days, but sometimes when it looked like it might rain, I had to wear it--not without argument. Sometimes I won and sometimes not.

I remember one afternoon coming home from school, and as I came through the field where the horses were grazing, they spied me in my black apparel and snorted in fear and came galloping straight for me. I stood rooted in my tracks and figured I was a goner for sure, but at the last minute the horses split, and one horse went by me on the left and the other on the right. I guess a guardian angel was watching over both me and the raincoat because we both survived.

After a few years I bought myself a nice blue rain jacket. This should have solved my problem so that I could retire the old coat that never wore out and that I never grew into. Not so. My pa said, "Your new coat is too short. You're going to get wet from the waist down." Well, I wore the old coat less and less, and with school days over I hung it out in the old shed with a sigh of relief--sight unseen and forgotten.

One day when I was heading to the pasture to get the cows, Pa's voice asked, "Where's your rain coat?"

"In the shed somewhere," I answered.

"Well, go get it."

I groaned as I went in search of it. Only the cows would see me now, but undoubtedly I'd scare the milk out of them. But as I reached for the old raincoat, I realized that a miracle had happened. As I held the coat, I noticed that it was riddled with holes. Some tiny rodents had chewed it so that it looked like a sieve. Hallelujah! Bless the little mice. My old rain coat was now gone for good.

Florence Edwardson

I don't know the moral of this story. Perhaps it means that if you have patience you will get what you want--even if it takes years and years.

Florence Edwardson lives in Whalen--population 80. She retired from work on a mink farm and now works at a resort. She enjoys nature, reading, and writing letters.

Mama's Good Dishes
by Julie Westrum King

I can't pass a second-hand store or an antique shop without a quick look for that pattern. Mother tells me now that she would have held on to them if she'd known how much those dishes meant to me. I believe her, but it never occurred to me to say anything at the time. She's looking in shops and at rummage sales too. Maybe one of us will find a set one day, maybe not. Maybe what I'm looking for can't be found in any second-hand store, and can't be bought at any price.

Daddy rolls up his shirt sleeves, and the uncles follow suit. The house is warm, and everyone is smiling, except Grandpa. He reigns supreme from the plush throne armchair next to the Christmas tree in the corner, his stockinged feet crossed comfortably on the hassock in front of him. The prickly hassock is so big that there is room enough for one little dark-haired, big-eyed girl to perch on a corner and tease Grandpa about his smelly feet. They don't smell, of course, but when I tease Grandpa, sometimes he gives me a sideways look that makes his eyes twinkle, and he smiles around his pipe with a one-sided wisp of a grin that I am sure is only meant for me, and no one else can see it. He pretends to ignore me and nods solemnly at one of his burly sons who has just made a loud point about something. The uncles always make their points loudly, and so do some of the aunts. Someday I will too.

We sit down to dinner at Mama's dressed-up dining room table. She uses her best table cloth and matching napkins. The napkins don't all really match (Mama made extras from piece goods, and the pattern is a little different) but everyone has a real cloth napkin and a little glass filled with dark Mogan David. Mama never uses centerpieces; the food itself decorates her table: steaming platters and bowls of rich feast day colors-- Hubbard squash, scalloped corn, cranberry relish, roasted meat, snowy mashed potatoes, golden rolls. But best of all, on Mama's table are the beautiful plates that hold the bounty, the bowls we pass among ourselves, the cups that radiate the aromatic message that dessert in on its way.

The day before Christmas Eve, Mama takes the good dishes out of the china cupboard and washes and dries them carefully. "Why do we wash the dishes before we eat, Mama?" I ask. She smiles and chuckles at her youngest, and though I am only 4, hands me a fresh hand-embroidered dish towel saying, "You can help dry the little plates if you're careful."

I am not always careful, but still she trusts me today. When we finish, she hugs me and says, "You are my good little helper." Mama's good dishes are the prettiest in the world. They are the creamy color of my favorite mashed potatoes, edged with the luscious deep glow of tart cranberry jelly, and in the center, like a gift, appears the tiniest bouquet of wildflowers when I have cleaned my plate like a good girl. When the dining room table is set with these dishes, I know good things are in store for this little one. And I don't have to wait long. The doorbell rings, and the tidy house fills with aunts and uncles, and the lamps are lit one by one, and the windows steam over with laughter, and cooking, and life.

Later I will lie awake in my little room over the kitchen, listening to the soft clinking and clicking of the aunts just below me, washing Mama's good dishes. "You cooked all day, Marina," they'll say, "now, you sit with Mother and keep us company while we clean up." And when I hear the solid stick of the china cupboard latch, I know Mama's good dishes are safe and waiting for next time. Then I can sleep.

Mother and Dad had moved three times at least before I was born, not counting the time Dad spent in the Army. By the time I was 8, I could remember living in four different houses. At that time, we were living in the third house in the second town of my childhood; but I knew it was time to move again the day Mother salvaged a couple of heavy cardboard barrels discarded by the laundry next door.

"These are perfect for packing dishes. The small one should hold all the good dishes and glasses!" she exclaimed. And it did. We moved back to the first town of my childhood, and after we unpacked, Mother stored those barrels in a dry part of the basement. She knew she would use them again, and she did, probably ten times before the big one wore out. She still had the small one twenty-five years later when she moved into the Senior Towers.

The good dishes only made two moves in those barrels. When I was in seventh grade, we moved from the tree-lined shores of southern Minnesota lakes to the wind-blasted endless prairies of South Dakota. We had to sell everything that wouldn't fit into a U-Haul trailer. We were broke, and whatever could be made on the moving sale, plus a loan from Grandpa, would set us up in the new place out west.

I never questioned why we had to move so much. I just accepted that our family was different. I secretly enjoyed explaining to new kids that my dad was a golf pro, and I cultivated the phrase, "You know, golf pros move around a lot, like preachers." I hated each move, but this move was the worst. In the months leading up to moving day, the air at home emanated tension like a sour smell. Dad broke into a rage over anything, and Mother went around with her lips held tightly together.

Buddy was away at college, and I was alone in a whirlwind of wrath and disapproval. Dad kept yelling things like, "What the hell's the matter with you these days!" and "Turn down that darned radio!" He didn't want to take me hunting anymore, and he complained all the time about me tying up the phone. I couldn't do anything right. My hair was ugly, and my face broke out. The world was against me.

The morning of the moving sale, the aunts, Mother and I set things up and tacked signs up around the neighborhood. My throat constricted as I watched Mother display her good dishes on a table in the front room, along with the other items for sale. I surreptitiously watched as ladies came and went, buying this or that. It didn't take long for a buyer to choose those dishes. "They're just coupon dishes, but I always liked the pattern," I heard Mother say to the lady who was offering her money from a large pocketbook.

"They're not for sale!" I wanted to scream. "Mama, don't sell them, please," I whispered to myself. But the lady walked out the door with a cardboard carton under her arm, and I never saw Mama's good dishes again.

I watched her move down the front walk, place the carton in the trunk of her car, and drive away. I realized my nose was pressed hard against the screen door, and it seemed hard to breathe. Turning away, I pivoted on one foot so fast the scatter rug flew across the foyer and tangled with the radiator. I ran up the stairs, holding tightly to the banister, sure I would throw up before I got to the bathroom.

But I didn't throw up at all. I slumped on the cold tile floor and cradled the cool porcelain in my arms while an emptiness slowly settled in my heaving stomach. As my face cooled and my breathing stilled, I raised my head and took a deep calming breath. Resolutely I got up and washed my face. Instead of going back downstairs, I went into my room at the end of the hall and closed the door behind me. I didn't want to help with the sale anymore.

We moved soon after that. I hated South Dakota. I hated the dinky trailer we lived in, I hated the school I went to, and I hated the kids I hung around the trailer park with. Mostly I hated my Dad for bringing us to this god-awful place. There were no trees, and the wind blew all the time. Everything was brown and ugly, especially me. That summer I went to work for the first time, washing clubs in the bag room behind Dad's pro shop. He paid me seven dollars a week, and I got Mondays off.

Each summer Dad gave me a raise and a little more responsibility. I filled in at the snack bar now and then, relieving somebody for lunch or a break. I sold Milky Ways and Popsicles to the members' tan and dripping children as they obediently tracked back and forth from Mommies to pool to snacks and back again. I studied the ones my age longingly as they roared up in the parking lot by the carful, played a round of golf, or lolled at the pool, charging lunch to their fathers' accounts. It wasn't their wealth or possessions I envied, as Dad thought and frequently railed at me about. No, it wasn't their money I coveted--it was their leisure time. It was their lazy afternoons, their companionable sultry evenings, their snoozy mornings I craved.

By the time I graduated from high school, I was a country club veteran. I could run the pro shop any day of the week, handle the stag day Best Ball, keep the scoreboard for the Pro-Am, make great coffee and whip up a ladies' day luncheon. Yet, when I reflect on my accomplishments, it is not with joy or pride or even fondness. I would have traded it all for a few more years of childhood, a few more lazy summer days, or even a few more Christmas Eve dinners on Mama's good dishes.

Julie Westrum King was born in Albert Lea and lived in Faribault, New Ulm, Sioux Falls, and Sheldon. She has one daughter and teaches speech, English and drama at Wauwatosa West High School in Wisconsin.

Setting Pins
Donald Matejcek

My grandson wanted to take us out for a treat on his birthday this year so we all spent an evening at the bowling alley. We had a lot of fun, and the experience brought back memories of my first paying job as a pin setter in Owatonna back in the 50's, when I was about my grandson's age. The main thing I noticed is that bowling has changed dramatically over the years.

Boys as young as 10 could earn money as pin setters when I was a kid. Like caddies, pin setters showed up at the job hoping but not knowing they would earn some money. Their salary depended on how much work they did.

Bowling alleys opened in the afternoon for some ladies' leagues and stayed open late. With their long hours of operation, they needed quite a few kids to set pins. I had experience working in Mom's grocery store, but store work was a family responsibility with no wages, and I wanted to work at the bowling alley so that I'd have some spending money. Since I was only 10, Mom allowed me to work only weekend afternoons.

The bowling alley in those days attracted kids who were labeled rowdy by small town standards, and it was considered by some to be a disreputable hangout. This led some parents to be wary of letting their boys work there, but we pin setters did not usually mingle with customers.

Hanging out with other pin setters was one of the fringe benefits. When we weren't working, we sat back behind the lanes and talked. Younger kids looked to the older guys, who were more skilled and could work faster. If business was really slow, we were tempted to go out into the lobby, where a seductive pinball machine promised a free game to anyone who could rack up a high score. Of course, spending money on pinball play cut into our profits.

The old Owatonna bowling alley is now the Elks club. We had six to eight lanes, and by the time I was old enough to work, the game had adopted some automation. In times before that, pin setters had to carefully place each pin on a mark painted on the floor. This allowed for some variance in each set-up. By the time I got the job, bowling had been automated a little, making the job somewhat easier than it had been.

We sat in a little boxed-off area above the gutter, separated from flying pins by a metal partition that resembled a cattle stanchion. We sat on the side of that partition with our feet up to protect them from getting hit by heavy bowling balls. Even with these precautions, we sometimes got bruised on our arms and legs by flying pins. We had to stay on our toes and hope the bowlers were paying attention and were not trying to make our lives difficult. Most of all, we had to learn to get the job done quickly while staying out of harm's way.

After a bowler rolled a ball, pins would fall into a shallow pit, spin on the floor or roll into the gutter. Pin setters would hop down and clear the alley for the next ball, taking care to avoid any pins still standing. Bowlers could see us reaching out to do our jobs, but occasionally their impatience or impudence would cause them to cast caution aside and throw their second ball before a setter finished clearing the fallen pins. Fortunately we could hear those balls rolling down the lane, and we had a few seconds to get out of the way.

Our bowling alley had a semi-automatic setter, but we had to load and operate it. We'd pick up scattered pins and set them up in a rack that had indentations for perfect pattern formation. When we pulled a lever, the loaded rack came down about two feet to the floor and released the pins on the lane in perfect order. Then the empty rack went back up to wait for us to load and lower the next set-up.

Some of the older guys got so good that they could do three or four lanes at a time. Being able to work so fast required a combination of concentration, agility, timing and speed that we younger kids admired. Not only was it neat to see someone working that efficiently, but those who could do more work got more pay. I can't remember exactly, but we got paid about ten cents a game. We filled out a card each time we worked to show how many games we had set, and at the end of a week we'd get paid. If the crowd was big, or if it was league night, a kid could earn pretty good money. If the crowd was thin, a kid could go home empty handed.

Bowling was a popular sport in those days. Professional bowling was broadcast on television every Sunday afternoon, and fans recognized the names and faces of several top bowlers. Kids learned how to bowl and keep score as part of their physical education classes, and lots of people owned their own bowling balls and shoes. A perfect 300 game was rare, even among pros.

When Brunswick invented automatic pin setters, some bowling alleys invested a lot of money and increased business because automation speeded the game and enabled bowlers to play more games per hour. Other alleys that couldn't afford the investment closed. Ten year old boys who wanted to earn a few bucks had to shovel snow or mow lawns.

Nowadays we have pop-up gutters and computerized scoring. It's possible to play the game without knowing how to score. Perfect games have become common because of the recent addition of pop-up gutters. The new places are not hangouts like the bowling alley I remember, and I noticed lots of families bowling together the night we were there, something I don't remember from the past. Another thing that has changed quite a bit is the price. We spent fifteen to eighteen dollars apiece when we each bowled a couple of games with my grandson, a far cry from yesterday when a dollar or two would pay for three or four games of bowling and equipment rental.

Don Matejcek is a fleet maintenance technician for Owatonna Public Utilities. In 1963 he was a founding member of the Owatonna Diving Club, one of the Midwest's largest and most active SCUBA organizations.

Architectural Landmark
by Kathy A. Megyeri

"Why is it that when we are young we don't go to the place
where we know we ought to go?" Carl Bennett

My entire youth was spent in Owatonna, but it wasn't until I was
60 years old and returned home in the company of an art history professor
that I toured America's most famous small-town bank building only one
mile from where I grew up. The National Farmer's Bank Building has
been recognized internationally as an architectural masterpiece since it
opened in 1908, and it was recently featured on a U.S. postage stamp.
But as a kid pedaling my bike down Cedar Street, I barely looked up at
this stone, brick, terra cotta, iron and stained glass monument. Most kids
paid little attention to the town's history and took the bank for granted.

At the time of construction, Owatonna was an especially productive
dairy region. Steele County, home of Owatonna, had twenty-one
creameries, and in the sixteen square miles that surrounded the town,
more butter was produced than in any other region in the U.S. The town's
most famous export was the mechanical butter churn, which was invented
in 1889 and which revolutionized the entire dairy industry. Thus, Owatonna
advertised itself as the Butter Capital of the World.

In 1906, Owatonna's 5,500 inhabitants were served by two
railroads, dozens of retail stores, four hotels, three banks, an automobile
factory and several manufacturing plants. The most pressing social issue
for the Germans, Czechs, and Scandinavians who founded the town in
1855 was prohibition. In its heyday, Owatonna boasted a public library, a
1200 seat opera house and the Beethoven Society choral group.

At that time, Carl Bennett, an Owatonna banker, was searching for
an architect who could design a new bank that would be different from the
usual columned Roman style banks. Bennett also wanted to attract new
customers and make even more money by emphasizing a secure, safe place
to keep money. In a leap of faith, Bennett hired 50-year-old Louis Sullivan,
who had been a pioneer in designing early skyscrapers but who was then
out of work and had never designed a bank. In hiring Sullivan, Bennett
also acquired the services of George Elmslie, chief draftsman in Sullivan's

office and a masterful ornamentalist. The threesome of Bennett, Sullivan, and Elmslie proved to be a magical combination.

After one year of attending MIT, Sullivan became an apprentice in Philadelphia and then traveled to France to enroll in the best architecture school of Ecole des Beaux-Artes, where he claimed to have learned "logical thinking." His career blossomed in Chicago after the 1871 fire, and the Wainwright Building that he designed in St. Louis was the first all-steel frame skyscraper with fireproofing and an elevator.

In the early 1890's, Sullivan was Chicago's most famous architect who mentored a new employee, Frank Lloyd Wright, but in 1906, Sullivan was recently divorced, out-of-work, fighting alcoholism, and suffering from criticism that his work was dated. His rigid and abrasive personality, his inability to deal with people, and his disregard for the feelings of others were his greatest faults that he openly admitted to. He wrote, "The simple, fundamental trouble that has caused all my unhappiness, bitterness, misery…is none other than my persistent lack of kindly feelings toward my fellow men."

Sullivan was also a man of contrasts: he lived like an aristocrat but preached democracy; he professed contempt for book learning, but wrote reams of dense prose and convoluted poetry and referred to himself in the third person; he designed scores of Chicago buildings but derided the city's materialism and called it "the growl of a glutton hunt for the dollar;" he showed little interest in designing for the working man in that his work was ornate and expensive, but still demanded that his pieces meet the needs of the common man; and he believed that architectural form should follow function, meaning that the design of a building should always flow organically from a building's purpose or use, but he also wrote that "buildings' ultimate function was spiritual in nature." Because he loved botany, his large, commercial buildings were heavily ornamented with stylized versions of plants.

Sullivan's chief draftsman, a Scotsman named George Grant Elmslie, was shy, sensitive, impractical, had terrible bouts of depression but had an unusual gift for ornamentation, so much so that copies of the Owatonna bank's terra-cotta ornaments were sent to the Louvre, probably the only time part of Minnesota architecture has been ever sent to Paris.

Fortunately for Sullivan, Owatonna's saloons were open for business when he made his first visit in 1906, and Bennett was impressed enough with his ideas to hire him.   In 1907-08, the bank was built by Hammel Brothers and Anderson, an Owatonna construction firm, on a site facing Central Park, directly across from the court house.   The bank cost $125,000 to build, an exorbitant amount at that time considering the nearby Carnegie Library cost only $32,000. The bank was the largest in the city—almost sixty-eight feet square and forty-nine feet high.   It resembles a giant ornamental treasure chest.   Its cube shape is punctured by two large arched windows, but the building is filled with ornamentation so beautiful and varied that it was the collective professional keystone for all three men and pivotal in their careers.   Sullivan called it a " color symphony" with burgundy and multicolored tapestry brick, green and brown terra cotta, blue and gold glass mosaics, black Belgian marble, pink sandstone, and two hundred shades of color harmonized by blue-green light that filters through stained glass windows.   In January of 1912, twenty-five strangers a day came to see it.

The bank, for Sullivan and Elmslie, garnered other bank commissions in small towns, most notably the Merchants Bank of Winona in 1912.   Although Bennett remained a banker, he started a fifteen-year period of advancing this "new architecture."   In 1920, farm foreclosures increased after the war had ended, and price supports fell, so in 1929, the bank was auctioned off to Owatonnans Carrie, Mark and Donald Alexander for $63,000 and then sold to Security State Bank for $35,000.

In 1940, more and much needed office space spurred a senseless remodeling that altered the floor plan and eliminated much of the rich ornamentation, most specifically the tellers' wickets that ended up as scrap metal or fell into the hands of private collectors.

The bank's original interior

In 1958, bank president Clifford Sommer attempted to return the bank to much of its former splendor while still insisting that it remain functional for increasing business needs. This renovation was so successful that Ivy Baker Priest, Treasurer of the U.S., attended the bank's rededication.

Today the bank still stands as a testimonial to Sullivan's belief that "As you are, so are your buildings. Architecture is a means by which human beings express their aspirations and ideals. They also reveal the shape of the past and means of ennobling everyday life."

As Owatonna celebrates its sesquicentennial next year, I'll return again to see the landmark that made my hometown famous. I'll photograph the large murals on the inside walls that depict pastures of cows that commemorate the once-powerful dairy business, and I'll admire the bank's ornamentation with new understanding. Then I'll silently thank Bennett, Sullivan and Elmslie for their gift to the city and to the architectural community and pray that other Owatonnans like me don't wait almost half a century to appreciate such beauty in their midst.

National Farmers Bank during construction in Owatonna, 1908

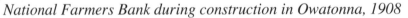

Kottke's Girls
By Kathy A. Megyeri

"The importance of jewelry is emotional and psychological—
we are all temporary custodians of beauty." Elizabeth Taylor

One's first real paying job has a profound effect on one's life, and
mine was no exception. In an attempt to instill the German work-ethic
that my parents were so proud of, my mother requested of the owner of
Owatonna's foremost jewelry store that I be allowed to work a couple
hours each day after school so that I would "stay out of trouble."

Carl. F. Kottke, the dignified and cultured owner of Kottke's
Jewelers on North Cedar Street, paid me 45 cents an hour to wash the
china displays on the second floor, arrange seasonal window displays,
wrap gifts, set up bridal registries, polish silver on the first floor, and catalog
and organize the basement warehouse so that we could find matches of
Reed and Barton silver, Fostoria glassware, and Bavarian china patterns
that customers wanted to replace their damaged or lost pieces.

Even back in 1958 when I started, the store was locked in a time-
warp. Two watch repairmen wearing magnifying eyeglasses sat behind
cluttered desks and assembled springs, stems, and watchbands into
functional, wearable timepieces. Kottke himself engraved initials into
wedding bands, sized rings, and replaced broken prongs that held precious
stones in place.

Giant showcases lined the store's walls. A muted linoleum floor
made nightly cleaning of snow and mud possible, and a pressed tin ceiling
from which long stemmed lights hung made this cavern of jewels, silver
and gold romantic and desirable. Only the huge, heavy, ornate safe on the
left wall was off-limits to young help like me.

When the front door opened, a small bell attached to the armature
would tinkle to announce "customer," and I would scurry up front to ask if
I could be of assistance. If a couple expressed interest in obtaining an
engagement ring, I would run back to fetch Mr. Kottke. He would scurry
to the front of the store dressed impeccably in a three-piece suit, with a

diamond stickpin in his tie and Rotary pin in his lapel.   He would
ceremoniously unlock the vault, slide out three or four trays of sparkling
diamond rings in all shapes and sizes that were cosseted in black velvet
lining, and with a flourish, show each tantalizing treasure to his rapt
audience.

Meanwhile, I would return to my washing, polishing, cleaning, or
organizing duties, and surreptitiously sneak looks at the usually shy guy
and the excited, giddy girl.   Mr. Kottke would take his time with each
couple, gently hold out one offering at a time, and quietly speak of facets,
clarity, cut and style while sizing up the man's ability to pay.   Finally he
would discount the purchase enough so that the buyer could see his way
clear to make the monthly payments.   This scene made me an incurable
romantic and had an enormous impact upon me in the following ways.

Although home entertaining has changed over the years and bridal
registration has lessened with time, I still note silver and dish patterns
whenever I travel or eat out.   Now, brides seem to opt more for pottery
than patterns, stainless steel instead of silver plate or sterling, and hand-
thrown goblets instead of crystal.   Lately, however, I've noticed a
resurgence in obtaining 50's pounded aluminum serving pieces, so maybe
silver and crystal will become trendy again in time.   Certainly, the elegant
five-piece silver tea and coffee service sets connote elegance in entertaining
and dining, so maybe another Kottke girl is now polishing those remaining
trays and pitchers still on display.

The Mall of America, sixty-five miles to the north and the super-
sized Walmart, a mile north of town have siphoned off business, but the
store, now run by Kottke look-alike son Bill, still offers service and
attention to detail.

I appreciate, now more than ever, the role the store has played in
the development of the community.   Both father and son have sold high
school football tickets, supported innumerable fund raisers for band
uniforms and choir robes, loaned store displays for local theater props,
taken up special collections for families who suffered from fires and floods,
boosted town events like the centennial and county fair celebrations,
contributed to funding the July 4th fireworks, and even provided an
informal meeting place in their back room for the town fathers to discuss

floating another bond or improving the" beltway" around the city. Kottke's role in boosting civic pride and fostering the feeling that merchants care about their customers can never be replaced.

That unique store taught me the importance of a stable and loyal client base and the value of a happy work force. When Mrs. Vita Alexander brought in her diamonds for cleaning, the whole store snapped to attention, in part because we knew hers were the biggest and best in town, and she'd probably soon buy another. When I graduated from high school, Carl Kottke home delivered a gold circle pin flush with salt-water pearls set around the circumference. I still have that piece and treasure it because my boss made me feel important and valued.

And then, there was the legacy of being a Kottke girl. We weren't just store clerks; we were special. My predecessors were Bobbie Bozoske, the 1958 homecoming queen, and the optometrist's daughter, Peggy Lundquist. My successor was Sue Engel, one of the most talented artists to graduate from high school. And once we graduated, went away to college, got married and had families, we came back to see if the store was physically the same as we hoped it would be, and to make sure the next Kottke girl was " up to snuff."

Granted, the two watchmakers retired when fine watches were replaced with $10 Timexes and batteries, but the store still celebrated the most major life events of births, marriages, birthdays, and Christmas gift-giving in special ways. The same long table sat in the middle of the store to feature suggested gift items, the bell still tinkled over the front door as customers entered, and if one looked long enough in that basement depository, a replacement salad fork in a silver Gorham pattern could probably be found for the one chewed up in the garbage disposal.

One of my fondest memories is working late at Kottke's on Christmas Eve, when the local farmer who suddenly remembered that he had no gift for his wife appeared just before closing and would buy just about anything and have it gift wrapped so he could return to milking his cows before it got too late. That farmer was assured that his wife would like his selection because even though I was only a teen, I helped him choose it, and after all, it came from Kottke's, the premier jewelry store in Owatonna.

Because of my first job at Kottke's, I have noticed, appreciated and wanted to acquire beautiful and outstanding pieces of jewelry. Just as dentists probably focus on people's teeth, I, like a radar scope, lock on to people's jewelry, be it a ring, watch, pin or earrings, the bigger and more exquisite, the better. And I've become a collector myself—big, chunky, quality pieces that make people notice me, an Elizabeth Taylor wannnabe with the wallet of a retired schoolteacher.

But as the years pass and I face my own mortality, I realize what Elizabeth Taylor meant when she wrote, " Having jewelry is a temporary gift—we owners are just the caretakers. We are only the guardians." Someone else will discover and enjoy the pieces I've come to collect and love over the years.

Because of Kottke's Jewelry Store, I feel the permanence of beauty that Liz felt when she wrote, " Just like the Duchess of Windsor's collection, my pieces will all be up for auction one day. They will be scattered to the four corners of the world, and I hope whoever buys each piece loves it as much as I do and takes care of it." For me, that's the joy of being a Kottke girl and part of the store's legacy.

Kathy Megyeri grew up in Owatonna and taught English in Maryland for 35 years. She has contributed articles and stories to many journals and publications and has presented workshops for the National Council of Teachers of English. She co-authored the first Minnesota Memories.

Farmer Jeans
by David J. Chrz

I buy all my own clothes-- always have, always will.   This was not the case with my parents, however, as my Mom bought all my dad's clothes-- socks, underwear, the whole shebang. With that keen eye that moms seem to have, she invariably got the sizes right, and Dad was generally satisfied with whatever she picked out for him.

This was not the case with his jeans, however.   The jeans my Mom brought home for Dad were the kind I still buy when I buy jeans-- fairly heavy material, blue denim, something like Levi or Lee or Wrangler currently offer.

We lived on a farm, and Dad was definitely not satisfied with those "town-guy" jeans. He wanted "farmer jeans--the kind with a pliers pocket." Each time she came home with jeans for him, Mom had to listen to that same "town-guy/farmer jeans-the kind with a pliers pocket" complaint.

Finally, one Saturday morning Mom went to the local farm store, the only place where "farmer jeans-the kind with a pliers pocket" were readily available, bought two pair, and brought them home for Dad.   He and I had been working down in the barn, and when we came in for lunch, Mom informed him of her purchase.   You would have thought it was Christmas by the look on his face; he literally rushed to his bedroom to put a pair on, while the rest of the family sat down to lunch at the kitchen table.

To say that my dad was not given to frivolity would be a gross understatement; even my hooligan teenage friends were scared to death of him.   He was of medium height, muscular, and starting to show the early signs of a little paunch.   As much as anything, his severe demeanor made him an imposing figure.

When he got his new jeans on, sure enough, they were just what he wanted-- lighter material, baggier cut, and with the requisite pliers pocket. Unbelievable as it seems to this day, knowing Dad's stern disposition, my mom, sisters and I sat at the table in shock as he entered the kitchen modeling his new pants.   Our kitchen was long and narrow, table at one end, sink and cabinets along one wall, and appliances along the other.   Here came Dad, new pants, no shirt, sweaty, hairy belly, and in the middle of the kitchen, he put an index finger on his head, leaped, and did a 360 degree pirouette in mid air.

RRRIIIPP!!   There, limp and lifeless, empty, never to know the joy of holding pliers, hung his beloved pliers pocket on the dishwasher handle.   Dad just stood there in disbelief, and finally mustered up a feeble "Well, Jesus Christ!"

It was a sad specter of the former man who, slump-shouldered, schlepped back to his room.   He put on his second pair of new "farmer jeans-the kind with a pliers pocket," went out the back door, down to the barn and back to work.   There were to be no more ballet exhibitions in our kitchen at the farm.

David Chrz grew up in Austin and graduated from Pacelli High School in 1965. He has lived in Abilene, Texas, since his discharge from the U.S. Airforce in 1975 and speaks with no trace of his former Minnesota accent.

Save the Last Dance
by David J Chrz

Living in one of the Northern tier states has a number of advantages, not the least of which is the opportunity to enjoy all four seasons. However enjoyable they might be, the long, cold winters in Minnesota can be particularly hard on farmers and their livestock.

We were a farm family, living ten miles east of Austin along the I-90 right-of-way. Like all our neighbors, we brought our cattle up into the barnyard, or "lot," as the pasture became dormant in late fall, and made preparations to feed hay to the cows all winter. During really harsh spells of winter weather, we kept them actually inside the barn, throwing down from the loft each day bales of straw for bedding, as well as bales of alfalfa or oat hay for feeding.

Cows being cows, and characteristically indiscriminate in their personal hygiene habits, a few days' worth of cattle in closed quarters required what my Dad euphemistically referred to as a "barn dance." With cows turned back out into the lot, we would heave to with pitchforks and manure spreader, making the barn ready for the next storm and its bovine boarders.

After I left for St. Mary's College, my Dad was short of readily available labor for this distasteful job so he would wait until it just HAD to be done and then phone me at school to schedule a barn dance ASAP, usually the following weekend. It was at first his great good fortune that many of my buddies in the dorm were from Chicago, and suckers for a "barn dance." It wasn't our fault that they had a severely skewed notion of what a barn dance actually was. Throw in the additional enticements of home cooking and laundry done by Mom--a person widely known to be good at this, even separating colors and everything-- and we had a ready and willing, albeit somewhat misinformed labor pool.

This all went swimmingly, until that clannish Chicago nature kicked in, and my buddies began to compare notes. After the true nature of one of Dad's "barn dances" was revealed, it became more difficult to find volunteers. They were still available, but the laundry and home-cooking antes had to be upped to nearly astronomical proportions.

Things rocked along like this for two winters. At the start of my junior year, I moved into a Winona apartment. By then most of my close friends were from Winona, and they were a tougher group to dupe. Minnesota boys were naturally skeptical of anything having to do with cows or barns.

My two closest friends were Sam and Burmy. When my Dad first called for a barn dance that winter, I just couldn't mislead them (that, and they wouldn't have fallen for it). I told them the whole ugly truth, and being true friends, they came home with me anyway. They already knew and liked my parents, and my folks really liked them, so I promised that after the barn dance we would have an especially enjoyable weekend. Little did I know…

Winona and Austin are about ninety miles apart so we left after class on Friday, and arrived (fortuitously) in time for supper. We got up Saturday morning and took up eating where we had left off the night before. Then after lunch, while my mother was buying groceries –lots of them- we started on our barn project.

Burmy was wearing a pair of work boots like Li'l Abner wore in the comic strip. They were about three-quarter, or ankle height, with real rounded toes. He referred to them all day while we worked as his "dancing slippers." This obscure reference had come about as a result of our decision the night before to go into Austin on Saturday night and go dancing at the Tower, a popular teen hangout. We had also considered Mark's Roller Rink in nearby Brownsdale, but decided on the Tower. Burmy insisted that he was going to wear that same pair of funky-looking boots when we went out dancing.

All afternoon as we worked in the barn, Sam and Burmy regaled my Dad with wild and totally improbable, if not outright impossible threats of what they were going to do with the Austin girls when they got to town that night. More than once I noticed my dad theatrically rolling his eyes as their descriptions became particularly outlandish.

After a long, cold, and windy afternoon of hard work interspersed with frequent snack breaks, we finished the barn dance, and after a huge supper, we began to get ready for a real dance.   Burmy showered first, and came downstairs in stocking feet, as he had left his dancing slippers outside where they belonged, given their condition. The rest of his ensemble consisted of jeans and a short-sleeved shirt with the special touch of a long-sleeved " long underwear" shirt underneath, the sleeves of which hung down below his outer shirt. This alone was really comical- looking and cracked up all of us, including my parents.

While Sam was showering and getting dressed, Burmy dealt with his dancing slippers. Our garden hose and a horse brush got them cleaned off enough, but they were soaking wet. Undaunted, he put the boots in my mom's oven to dry. (It is probably unnecessary to say, but I want it to go on the record here that my mom had absolutely no notion that this was going on.) The oven did the drying job splendidly, but had the additional and unexpected effect of curling the leather soles upwards, so that those rounded toes were pointing somewhere in the vicinity of Burmy's forehead. This phenomenon was not readily reversible. Burmy had made such a production all day about his slippers that he was forced to have the courage of his convictions. So that was how he was dressed when we left for town.

When we reached the Tower, Sam and I fairly bounded up the long, two-flight stairway to the club, but Burmy was considerably slower coming up the stairs. Once inside, Sam and I wasted no time before asking girls to dance and getting started on the evening's entertainment. Burmy, however, found a warm, comfortable seat and promptly fell asleep.

All evening, as Sam and I danced with different partners, we disavowed any connection with or knowledge about the weirdo sleeping in the corner with the long underwear and elf boots. However, the jig was up at closing time when we had to go wake him up and let him hobble out to the car with us. After all the bold talk about his projected night on the town, I thought my Dad would have a cardiac arrest laughing when he heard Burmy's actual story the next morning.

All in all, it had been a good weekend. We left for Winona Sunday afternoon with full stomachs and clean clothes. The barn had been thoroughly cleaned. The Austin girls had once again narrowly escaped the ravages of the Winona contingent of Attila's army, and best of all, my dad had been given a story that he loved to tell the rest of his life.

Prairie River Cabin
by Richard Hall

After World War I, the logged-over lake country of northern Minnesota with its second growth timber was taking on a new look. Improved transportation led to more roads, freedom, independence and leisure. With automobile improvements and more people being able to afford them, the mood of the country was changing, and more people started to travel and enjoy the great outdoors.

Entertainment was a luxury, so people had to look for inexpensive or free leisure activities. There were family reunions or get-togethers, moonlight hayrides or sleigh rides, bonfires with wiener or marshmallow roasts, hunting, fishing, camping, and Sunday picnics in the park.

Because summers in the 1930's were so scorchingly hot, people spent a lot of time outdoors. On a hot summer day you would find crowds near the water where it was a little cooler.

During World War I, my grandfather Lew Hall was a foreman over several departments at Hormel in Austin. He had five children, and his number never came up in the draft. The influenza epidemic spread throughout the country, and my grandfather became sick and unable to work. There was no money coming in, so the Halls moved into a large house on Railway Street near the rail yards and the Hormel plant. My grandmother cooked for railroad section crews and the Halls took in boarders and rented rooms to railroad and Hormel workers.

My dad and uncle were just kids, but they got jobs at Hormel and paid board and room. Because of the war contracts, there were a lot of jobs in the packing industry. When my grandfather regained his health, he was offered a better paying job as a supervisor with a large packing company in St. Paul. He took the job, and my grandparents and their youngest son moved to St. Paul.

The new job brought more money and an improvement in lifestyle. Many stories could be written about how people found their way into the Arrowhead country of northern Minnesota, and this is just one of them.

It's hard for someone today to realize what a limited amount of products were available in the market during the 1930's. The military had used a lot of canvas during World War I. After the war, companies that made canvas turned to civilian consumers. Sears Roebuck and Montgomery Ward catalogs offered a large assortment of tents and other canvas products like tarps, chairs, and cots and enticed buyers with a purchase plan of a small down payment and monthly installments.

Large tents became popular, and some were as big as a small cabin. People purchased tents so that they could spend weekends and holidays camping in the great outdoors. The Halls bought a family size tent with wooden sections that fit together to make poles. The tent was high enough for adults to stand up inside, and had a divider down the center that formed two large rooms. It didn't have a floor so the Halls used canvas tarps to cover the ground. On the outer walls were windows with mosquito netting and an outer canvas flap. On the front was a large canvas flap that provided shade when raised and exposed a door with mosquito netting.

At first my grandparents did not venture far and did their fishing and camping at one of the small lakes near St. Paul. But after reading articles in the Sunday paper about the north woods and hearing about big fish in the northern lakes, they became more adventurous.

My grandfather was handy with tools and knew how to fix a broken-down car, so he would get together an assortment of tools and car parts, a tire pump, jack, oil, can of gas and drinking water. He would tie fishing poles on the side of the car and fasten his tackle box to the running board. Everything he couldn't fit in, he tied to the car. My grandmother took charge of packing food, clothing and bedding for their trips.

It wasn't uncommon for campers to find a nice campsite near a lake, river, woods or even outside a resort or picnic area and set up camp. Few felt they had to ask permission. If someone objected, they just moved to a different location. It was unusual for anyone to leave a mess. They would dig a hole and bury trash or burn it at their campfire.

The Halls made several trips and camped at different places until they got as far as Prairie River in Aitkin County. They chose for their campsite a clearing between the Prairie River and the road. Wooded all around with maple, birch, white and jack pine, the site was like wilderness. Fishing was good, and they enjoyed privacy, so they came back several times.

One day a man walked into their camp when my grandmother was fixing lunch. He said he was an agent for a company that owned the land and told them that it had been platted and was being sold. Several lots were for sale, and if they were interested in the one they were on, they could buy it. He said that if someone else bought the land, they would probably not be able to use it.

My grandmother wanted to know more about the lots. The man brought out a map that showed how his company had planned lots, roads, parks and public access to be developed along the Prairie River, Lake Minnewawa, and Indian Point.

They saw that this particular lot was bigger than most and that it extended from what was laid out to be a back road down to the shore of the Prairie River. It had a good growth of second timber and was one of the few lots with river shoreline. This campsite was like a second home to the Halls, and so in 1922 they bought it for $1000.

Like so many people in those days, the Halls went without when they couldn't pay for something. Since work was sometimes seasonal, people saved in good times so that they wouldn't have to go into debt during bad times. My grandparents thought the lot would be a good investment, and they thought they might eventually be able to replace their tent with a cabin if they did much of the work themselves. Several of the lots sold, but the development of the region was slow.

Money was scarce up north, and banks had little money to loan for cabins. Twin Cities banks weren't interested in investing outside that community so land development up north was difficult.

Most of the new northern land owners did a lot of hauling and built cabins themselves with the help of friends and relatives. Since there were no zoning laws, early cabins were more like one-room shelters built by fishermen, hunters or bachelors.

Some folks were able to convince lumber companies to carry them on their books while they made monthly payments and built or improved cabins. Others were able to build an entire cabin from scrap lumber or wood salvaged from old buildings being torn down. They loaded trucks or trailers or tied things to the tops of cars and hauled load after load from the cities or other places. With poor roads and tires, drivers spent a lot of time fixing flats and broken-down vehicles.

Most of the cabins were whatever design the owners or carpenters could come up with. Since they had nothing but hand tools and everything had to be hauled from a long distance, builders were limited as to what they could actually accomplish. Sometimes they hired professionals to hang doors, cut rafters, or install windows, but most cabin owners did their own construction work.

My grandparents eventually spent another $1000 for a small cabin, which was a lot of money in those days. They started with one room and covered the outside with heavy tar paper. Since they did not intend to be there during winter, the walls were not insulated. The inside walls were covered with a quarter inch pressed paper called hard board. They had a sink but no indoor plumbing, so water drained outside to a worm bed.

When they washed up, they used a blue enamel basin. On the outside of the cabin hung two wash tubs for bathing and laundry. Beside the sink was a white water pail with a dipper for drinking water. They used oil lamps, and about forty feet from the cabin was a two-hole outhouse.

Along one wall was a wood burning stove for cooking and heat. There was always a coffee pot and tea kettle for hot water on the stove. Behind the stove they hung pots and pans, and next to the stove they kept a large wood box well supplied. Calendars from the Great Northern Railroad hung on the walls, and they hung most of their clothes on hooks.

Eventually they added an adjoining windowed porch that served as two bedrooms. Two draw curtains hung on each side of a little center entry way, and each bedroom held a double bed and stand. They covered subfloors with four inch tongue and groove flooring and gave it a coat of dark stain but didn't varnish it. With the addition of the porch, the cabin now had front and back doors.

It's hard for me to comprehend what the life of my grandparents was like at the time when they built their cabin. With the short summer season, a full work week in St. Paul, little money, difficult travel back and forth on primitive roads in old cars, no phone or relatives in the area, cabin life was much different from today's getaways.

Three paths led from the Hall's cabin. One followed the dirt driveway west to the pump, then to the corner of the main road to the mailbox. Another path went east from the cabin through the trees where the Halls had a dock and rowboat. The third path went to where they had their outhouse and a chopping block and sawhorse for cutting stove wood. They only locked the place when they went back to St. Paul, and they never had trouble with vandalism.

When I was a little kid in Austin, I loved to hear about my grandparents' cabin. Because I was the oldest grandson, I enjoyed their fond attention, and they promised to take me up there for a fishing trip. When I was 9 years old, my mother's health was so bad she was unable to take care of my sister and me. My dad was working ten hour days, seven days a week so my grandma Chapman took my sister, and Grandma and Grandpa Hall picked me up so I could stay with them until school started.

I sat in the shade of a large elm tree every day waiting for my grandfather to come walking home from his job at the packing plant in St. Paul. He always wore a chambray shirt and bib overalls and carried a black lunch pail under his arm. That summer was scorching hot, and my grandmother kept the windows and doors open. My grandfather and I would walk into the kitchen, and he would put his lunch bucket on the table and tell me to check it out. It's hard to believe-- in an age when we have so much-- what an enjoyable experience that was. He would always save me an apple, slice of pie, or donut from his lunch.

After my grandfather rested and cleaned up, my grandmother would pack a picnic, and we would go out to the beach. While it was still light, I would wade and dog paddle with new-found friends. The boys wore old cutoff overalls for swimming, and the girls wore old dresses. When it got dark, we'd start a bonfire and roast wieners and marshmallows. Then we'd fish for bullheads, which bit so fast we sometimes all had bullheads on our hooks at the same time.

On hot summer days the farmers couldn't risk bringing livestock to market, so my dad would get home from work early. The Mississippi River was within easy walking distance, so we'd go to the Robert Street bridge. Those fish were mostly suckers, red horse and carp. If Grandpa caught a big fish, he would exchange poles to see if I could bring it in. He never saved any of those fish because in those days there were always down and out people along the river bank who wanted them.

One day my grandmother told me to go to bed early because we were going to go to the cabin early the next morning. I went to bed while it was still light and had a hard time getting to sleep. I had been looking forward to seeing the cabin for such a long time so I was very excited.

The next morning my grandparents packed their old Ford. On the running board my grandfather tied boxes and a suitcase. Long bamboo fishing poles were tied on the side. Everything was a new experience for me, and I was very excited. It was fun at first, riding in the rumble seat watching the Cities disappear. We seldom saw a car from either direction, and when a car passed, I had to get down in my seat and cover my head from the shower of dust and gravel from the highway. Then I would look back and see dust boiling up behind our car.

The sun rose high, and I was getting hot when my grandpa pulled the car off the road to a shady place for a picnic lunch. My grandparents knew I was tired of riding in the rumble seat by myself, but there wasn't much they could do. There was no room for me in the passenger compartment. The farther north we got, the fewer things there were to see. We passed through McGrath and McGreggor, and my grandmother remarked later that we never saw another person or even a dog.

Gas stations were few and far between, as were sign markers. Since cars used and lost more oil in those days, we stopped whenever we could to check the oil. The farther north we got, the worse the roads were. We passed more wilderness and pine trees until we came to a crossroad. There was a farmstead with a white house and lots of cows. On the front of a small building was a sign that said " Sather's Store." We stopped so that my grandmother could get fresh milk and eggs. To get to the door we had to drive though hay and weeds, even though they had a horse to try and keep the weeds down.

Sathers didn't have many customers so there were just some tracks through the weeds. They had one gas pump, and lots of white chickens cackled and darted around when we entered the store. Mrs. Sather greeted my grandmother like they were long lost friends. My grandfather took me to the back of the store where Mr. Sather helped him fill a fifty-five gallon drum of kerosene. Many shelves stood empty, as the Sathers stocked only necessities. The only light was what came in the window, and the wooden floor creaked with every step. There must have been days and weeks when nobody entered the store.

We followed old car tracks through tall weeds and traveled east down a narrow, winding dirt road, then turned north. The trees arched over the road and formed a cool canopy. When the road crested, I finally caught a glimpse of Lake Minnawawa through the trees.

Pretty soon we reached the Prairie River Bridge, where I saw Big Sandy Lake. My grandfather stopped the car on the bridge, and we got out so I could see where the Prairie River entered Big Sandy Lake. We traveled about a half mile and turned off onto what looked more like a wagon trail than a road. My grandfather turned off the road and drove alongside the door of a small cabin in the shade of the trees and stopped the car.

As tired as I was, I don't believe I even waited for the car to stop, and I was out and headed for the Prairie River I had heard my grandparents rave about. My actions caught my grandparents by surprise, but in no time my grandfather was behind me trying to catch up before something happened to me.

It has been over seventy years since I got my first glimpse of the scenic beauty and magnitude of the Prairie River flowage. My grandfather pointed out two large blue gray birds standing on one leg in the foliage on the other side. When they heard us, one flew off with a squawk.

As we stood there on the dock looking out over the beauty of the north country, a fish jumped, breaking the black, cold water. I got excited and wanted to go fishing right away, but my grandfather assured me there was plenty of time, and that the fish would still be there after we unloaded the car and ate supper.

When we got back to the cabin, my grandmother had the door and windows open to air the place out. After she washed everything, checked the mattress for mice, and unpacked their belongings, my grandfather restocked the cupboard shelves, filled the lamp, and shook the rugs. After we rested, my grandmother cooked a meal for us, and we took our bamboo poles and went fishing off the dock and along the shoreline. Inside the little cabin later, it was cozy with the dim light of the lamp. My grandfather opened an old army cot for me to sleep on, and I thought that was great. My dreams of going fishing again came true early the next morning.

Richard Hall, an Austin native, worked at Hormel, has written three books and has created hundreds of pen and ink drawings. He also designed props for The Matchbox Theater. He and his wife Mickie live in Rochester.

Prom Night, 1936
by Madonna Hazen Erkenbrack

"Are you going to the prom?" "Who are you going with?" The prom was all anyone talked about at school in International Falls that spring of 1936.

My dress was homemade--baby blue satin with a wide sash that tied in the back resembling a chic bustle. My mother and I went to J.C. Penney's in Internatonal Falls to select a very "in" style in Vogue's pattern book. The dress was the most elegant creation I had ever seen My mother banned me from her sewing room because I kept interrupting her. I wanted to be sure my dress would look exactly as it did on the pattern cover.

I came home from school one afternoom to hear my mother call me into her sewing room for the final fitting to be sure the floor length creation was the perfect length for my three inch heels. I felt like a princess when I saw myself in the mirror. The scooped neck made the shape of my face pretty, and the color brought out the blue of my young, bright eyes. My blonde hair was cut in the latest bob style. If I do say so myself, I looked gorgeous.

Three weeks earlier, I waited in the library for Bernard, who was unofficially courting me. He asked me to meet him in the library because he wanted to ask something special. I knew what he was going to ask, but I wasn't absolutely sure. All the girls were talking about the prom, and I wanted to go with Bernard, who had dark hair and was rather short. Being a woman of short stature, I could look right into his brown eyes. When he asked me, he whispered so the strict librarians didn't kick us out. I almost shouted with joy, but instead I smiled and quietly said, "Yes"

The prom was held in the school gymnasium, which was also the auditorium stage. Spectators paid 25 cents to view the exquisite affair. When Bernard and I entered the gym, I saw my classmates looking so beautiful, and yet I felt my Vogue dress was the best. None of the girls had corsages because it was the Depression, and no one could afford flowers. To give spectators a chance to see our dresses, we had a grand march. Couples lined up by height at the end of the gym and followed the center line until the boys turned to the right and the girls went to the left.

It was easy to dance to the music played by an all-accordion band. They played slow dreamy tunes, and we were so intent on having a good time that it was a magical night. Bernard held me at an appropriate distance as the chaperones beamed. We were all ladies and gentlemen. As Bernard escorted me to the punch and dessert table, he whispered, "I wish this night would never end, Madonna." Finally though, twelve o'clock came and we heard,"Good Night, Ladies." We knew our glorious prom had ended.

Bernard and I had permission to go to the family-rated midnight show at one of the three theatres in International Falls, For the life of me I can't remember the movie we saw. The fact that I can't remember the movie may sound a bit risque in this modern world, but what actually happened was that our Methodist minister came and sat next to me to keep an eye on all the prom goers. Sharing the arm rest with my minister was a traumatic experience for a girl out on her first grown up date.

After the movie, we went to the Chicago Cafe on Main Street, where we had my favorite treat, which was an ice cream parfait made with layers of strawberry, chocolate, vanilla -- at least four layers of ice cream-- topped with gobs of whipped cream and chopped nuts. It was as good as it sounds.

In the wee hours of the morning, Bernard drove his Dad's car back in front of my house.

Madonna Erkenbrack

With no time for parking or any hanky panky, he escorted me to the door and gently held my hand as we said good night. I knew Mother was awake and waiting for the creak of the steps and the click of the door.

The next day I had to attend church, but I couldn't look the minister in the eye because, I guess, I was rather angry at him for intruding in the dreamiest night of my life when I was acting like a sophisticated grown-up for probably the first time in my sixteen years. Minister or no minister, it was a night never to be forgotten.

Madonna Erkenbrack taught business education in Bricelyn and Austin, at Macalaster College and in California. She lives with her husband Don in Vallejo, California.

Laughter Therapy
by Arvin Rolfs

The term "laughter therapy" was officially coined by Norman Cousins in his 1979 book, *Anatomy of an Illness*, but I was using that same concept to my own benefit more than twenty years prior to that.

According to his account, Cousins was suffering from a degenerative disease of his body's connective tissues, and he was literally becoming unstuck. He began to suspect that the anti-inflammatory drugs and other pain-killers combined with hospital routine that disrupted his rest were actually contributing to his predicament. So with his doctor's cooperation, he took control of his own treatment.

By checking out of the hospital and into a full-service hotel, he was able to get undisturbed rest at a much lower cost. And he found that with ten minutes of hearty laughter translating into two hours of restful sleep, he was able to dispense with pain-killing drugs altogether. As such, belly-laughs were an integral part of his prescriptions, administered in generous doses of old Marx Brothers movies, Candid Camera TV clips, and selected readings of funny stories. Several months under that regimen enabled Cousins to leave the hotel, symptom-free from what the doctors had earlier diagnosed as an irreversible, terminal condition.

My case was a little different from that. I had contracted polio in 1948 at age 9 and spent about a year at the Sister Kenny Institute in Minneapolis. Another two-month stay in 1952 convinced me and my parents that enough of my childhood time had been spent in a hospital.

However, by the time I graduated from Luverne High School in 1957, I was enough of a realist to know that I needed help, big-time! Beyond benefiting any more from mere physical therapy, I was admitted to Gillette Children's Hospital in St. Paul in 1958 for a series of corrective surgery procedures and, following that, rehabilitation.

My final surgery, about six months into the whole treatment, really put me into the pits. I had been bedridden all those months, wearing a body cast because of spinal surgeries, but that didn't mean I wasn't in control of my turf. It was a rather limited turf by most standards, but I could manage every inch of it with the help of a trapeze bar over my bed. As long as I could maneuver in bed and reach my stuff in the stand along side it, I was content. But that last surgery changed everything.

The result was a long leg cast attached to the body cast, so I was in plaster from chin to toe. Like a turtle on its back, I couldn't move. There were three possible positions available to me, but someone had to put me there: 1. Flat on my back; 2. On one side with my opposite leg sticking up in the air at a 45 degree angle; 3. Flat on my stomach, lying crosswise on the bed so my face was free to breathe. The first was for sleeping, the second for looking about and visiting, and the third for eating, reading, writing and playing cribbage, with a chair bottom as my table top.

This was to be my existence for the next three to four months, and I didn't like the looks of it. After my parents left on visitors' day, life started to look sour and so did I. They had left me a book though, which was a little unusual because the hospital had a library full of books for kids to read. But they had seen the movie, *No Time for Sergeants*, starring Andy Griffith, found it really funny, and thought I'd enjoy the book.

Compared to most people, my sense of humor had always been rather subdued; I'd smile at something laughable, chuckle at something hilarious, or snort out a "hah hah" at something uproarious. But this book broke all norms and had me shaking with laughter. Since my body cast didn't leave much room for belly jostling, and since I was covered with plaster, when one part of my plastered body moved, all parts moved.

My "hah's" became "ha, ha, ha's" with no breaths between. A paragraph of laughter exhausted me. People passing in the hallways would stop in to see what all the hilarity was about. It was slow reading, though. I spent a lot of time on my back that week, recouping from laugh seizures.

On the morning of my surgeon's visit a week after my surgery, instead of a breakfast tray, the nurse brought me a surgery prep tray.

"Oh, didn't they tell you? she said. "The doctor wasn't satisfied with the job he did last week. He wants to work on you again, today."

" Great! A week wasted! Tack on another week to the eternity it'll take for me to get out of here!" was my response. After x-rays of my knee and an interminable time in the pre-surgery room, an orderly showed up and wheeled me back to my room. The doctor found my knee was properly set after all and canceled the surgery. Hallelujah! It must have been the belly laughs that jostled the bones into place.

I'm not sure Norman Cousins would include bone setting as one of the expected benefits of laughter therapy, but in my case it was a definite side benefit. For me, as for others like me, the real benefit of frequent and prolonged laughter was its affect on the attitude. Probably in time I would eventually have adjusted to my confined way of life, but laughter propelled me there on greased skids. And it was a fun trip!

Years later, I witnessed in my father's fight against Hodgekin's Disease the importance of attitude in coping with ill health. Friends of his from church remarked to me what a good spirit he maintained in the face of radiation and chemotherapy, as did his doctor. My mother told me the best medicine for his attitude was to have us kids come home on weekends. That gave him four good days out of the week to cope with the side effects of his treatment: Friday, looking forward to the weekend, the weekend itself, and Monday, remembering the weekend.

After all these years, after describing for my wife so frequently the virtues of what I have always considered the funniest book in the world, she recently bought me a copy of *No Time for Sergeants*. I have found, though, that either my sense of humor has changed over the years, or the book has. I now find it amusing, but no longer hilarious.

Tastes do change, and we all have different perceptions of what is funny. I still crack up over some Marx Brothers antics while my wife wonders if I ever will grow up. We both like Tim Conway's comedy sketches, though, and my stomach starts jiggling in laughter all over again as I recall some of his scenes. But good friends of ours think his videos are just dumb. What is a joke to some might well be a jerk to someone else, but whatever makes us laugh is always good therapy.

Arvin Rolfs, who grew up near Kenneth, is a computer systems analyst. He lives with his wife Nancy in Brooklyn Center.

Tekla
by Marilyn Mikulewicz Baranski

I have known only one Tekla, and she was my father's older sister. She was probably the cleanest and most conservative woman I have ever known--within reason. She said what she thought and did what she liked.

Tekla thought she would like a bright red ceiling in her kitchen, and by golly, her pristine, white Victorian kitchen got a bright red ceiling. I believe the color in that day and age was known as " Chinese red." I think she had the red ceiling about forty years because she said it made her happy. You have to imagine Tekla in her sensible shoes, her permed hair in a discreet hair net, and her simple plaid but well-ironed house dress covered by a large hand- made apron, cooking in her kitchen. Her house was a place where dust of any kind just wasn't allowed. I know that when she came to our house, she always smelled the dish rag, a habit that made my mother run for a fresh one as soon as we saw Tekla and her husband turn into our driveway.

Tekla and Leo came to our house every other Sunday about 1 p.m. after church and stayed until about 8 in the evening. In the afternoon on the good days, Tekla and I went to the garden to weed or just to see how things were growing. Each time I walked through the area where onions were planted, she sang to me, "Just a Lonely Little Petunia in the Onion Patch." Tek and I would walk past the barns, and she would comment on how great the air smelled--not like the air in the city. On a lot of Sundays, my father and Tekla would talk about old times and the generations before them. I so wish that I could hear those conversations again now when I am trying to find genealogical answers.

One time when they were climbing into their old Ford as they prepared to go home, a plane flew over, and Tekla looked up and said, "If the good Lord wanted us to fly, he would have given us wings." I looked at her feet and was going to comment that he didn't give us wheels either, but fortunately, the good Lord kept my mouth shut. We went back into our house and away from the mosquitoes and found a couple packs of gum which Leo always left above the cat cut-out where there were hooks for keys. He usually left Black Jack and Juicy Fruit, my favorites.

Tekla's hobbies included gardening, and each year she found a few of the latest or most unusual plants. Tekla brought us yellow raspberries and yellow tomatoes, which were really new back then and caused everyone to taste and retaste the unusual foods.

One time at our new farm, my father put in a lawn which was green and lovely. Then suddenly a few weeks later, we noticed these little plants with white flowers and yellow centers growing profusely in the lawn. During a dinner conversation about yards and lawns, my father mentioned how these little weeds were ruining his new grass. Without a note of apology in her voice, Tekla explained that she and Leo had come down one day when we weren't home and planted chamomile because she had noticed we had absolutely no chamomile, which makes the best tea when you are sick with flu or have a cold. My father was not pleased to hear this, to put it mildly.

She worked at her church, I think St. Adalbert's in St. Paul, for bingo every Saturday. Some of the women spent over $1OO a day on bingo, and she had to rush to sell cards in time for the next game. It was sinful, but the money went to the church. She washed clothes every Monday, which I guess most women did during that era, but not every woman described it with such gusto.

My aunt loved life and was tickled by cartoons. She told of one where someone made a lady scarecrow and put his wife's old dress on it. As time went on, a watermelon vine grew up the scarecrow's leg. Finally, a watermelon started to form in the stomach area of the scarecrow. A man walked by and scratched his head saying, "If I hadn't seen it, I wouldn't have believed it." Tekla told of that cartoon over and over and giggled so that we all laughed.

Way back when Tek was getting close to marriageable age, and she had met Leo, a young man from Wisconsin, it soon became apparent that he liked his liquor. I never heard her say anything about his past drinking, but I did hear an older relative say that Tekla told Leo to go away and come back in six months if he had totally stopped drinking.

From what I heard and saw, after Tekla told Leo to leave, he never had another drink for the rest of his life. He was a bald man with a rounded face, and he was a little deaf. In the summer he would take a white handkerchief and tie a knot in each corner and put it on his head so he wouldn't have a sunburned scalp.

He repaired sewing machines and even went to the big textile factories and designed ways to make their machines sew zippers and buttons. He was a clever man. He probably would have been famous or at least rich had it been a later time. He always brought us sacks of fabric remnants from which we could make skirts or pajamas- --or doll clothes.

Tekla Mikulewicz and Leo Kozlowski

Leo was always repairing something-- especially around their home. They had an old brass bed that I loved. Leo had found it in a second hand shop and bought it in a trade or for practically nothing, as it needed repair. They had some really neat things that Leo had repaired and brought back to life. They had a nice relationship together, and yet something was missing.

Tekla and Leo desperately wanted children. They decided that since the economics of the times were tight, they could only afford one child. The orphanage brought out two little boys from whom they were to choose. Tekla said it was the hardest decision of her life. Both little boys were so precious, but she and Leo were fearful of not being able to feed a second child.

Finally, they chose little Lawrence, who was the most wonderful son they could ever have had. He was the best man at my parents' wedding.

Lawrence and his beloved Italian wife Mary had two children, Marie and Diane, who all lived upstairs in their big Queen Ann Victorian at ll9 East Cook Avenue in St. Paul, where violets bloomed in the round lower turret windows, and delicious Italian spaghetti smells came out of the upstairs window. Tekla loved her family with every breath that was in her. And yet at every meal there was always an extra serving, just enough for the little boy she had left at the orphanage. She still wanted both little boys.

She had a heart of gold, yes, but she wasn't a little demure thing, either. I remember one time when there was a family gathering, and I came in wearing the latest style wig I knew made me look oh so glamorous and the next thing to a movie star, yet was so perfectly natural that no one would guess all that hair wasn't mine.

From across the room, Tek yelled out, "That wasn't the hair God gave you!" Yes, she was conservative--within reason.

Marilyn Mikulewicz Baranski grew up near Hastings, graduated from Winona State, and taught in California. She and her husband Fred have one adult daughter. She helped gather stories for this book from native Minnesotans who migrated to California.

Christmas on the Farm
by Marilyn Mikulewicz Baranski

My grandmother often said that time goes faster as you grow older. What I remember is that when you are a kid, waiting for Christmas takes forever.

Christmas started for us when the first catalog full of toys came in the mail. I can remember looking at each of the dolls in the catalog to see which ones would make the best babies and which were the most beautiful. I think I learned to measure by reading the dimensions of each baby and figuring out if it would feel like a real baby in my arms. I would go through all the catalogs and circle everything and anything my heart desired. By the time Christmas came, very little remained uncircled. My father would tell me, "Santa can't bring everything. He has to save some of the toys for the other little boys and girls."

A couple of times we went to some big building in Hastings or South St. Paul to see Santa. I don't know where we were, as there were a zillion people waiting in lines that went on forever. Everybody was taller than I was, and I was between a mass of moving overcoats. I remember telling Santa how good I was, and then feeling a little guilty because I really hadn't been totally perfect. Waiting in that long line, I would rehearse what I had to tell Santa. I was only allowed to tell Santa four things that I really, really wanted. I then had to tell Santa a couple of things for my brother too, because he was too little to stand in those long lines. Each year I wrote a letter to Santa-- just to be sure he didn't forget my list.

About a week before Christmas, the ornament box came down from the attic, and a tree arrived in the house. One year we had two trees because my father had planted a windbreak of fir trees on our property. Other people helped themselves to our trees too, unfortunately. We cut our trees because a few had been planted too close together. That was the first year we had bubble lights and fake snow from a can.

Our trees were glorious. One of the trees sat on a small table covered by a white sheet. The ornament I had made at school was exquisite, of course. In my eyes all my ornaments made our trees the beauties they were. I can still close my eyes and smell the spicy, fresh pine fragrance. I remember the lights, the bubbles and the shiny balls. I was disappointed that all the ornaments didn't light up. There could never be too much sparkle at Christmas.

A few days before Christmas, Mom scrubbed the old baby bathtub for fruitcake mixing. My mother measured ingredients, and my father stirred. I always wanted to taste the candied fruit, but I didn't like it, as it was too sweet. My father put wax paper in every bread pan we owned, and my mother filled each pan with batter. A new fad one year involved baking batter in old tin vegetable and soup cans so you would end up with solid cylindrical cakes. I haven't recently seen people do this --and there must be a reason. We made cut-out sugar cookies with red and green sprinkles and spritz cookies with sprinkles and little silver edible pearls. We were ready when people dropped by and when Santa came too.

On the day of December 24, I busied myself cleaning house because I wanted Santa to see me being super good when he peeked through the window. I also reviewed the Christmas catalogs again just in case I changed my mind. I wrapped my gifts to the family-- or rather put bows on the packages that had been pre-wrapped in Our Own Hardware and the Ben Franklin variety store. I don't think any of us knew about real wrapping paper.

We ate early on Christmas Eve. As it was beginning to become dark, we bathed and put on our pajamas. We turned on the news, just in case there were any Santa sightings. Cedric Adams on WCCO radio always reported the latest.

My father left to go to the barn and milk cows-- promising to hurry so he wouldn't miss Santa. My mother read " 'T was the Night Before Christmas" to us, and then we had to position ourselves to look out the back bedroom window to see if we saw Santa and his reindeer. We couldn't move or leave that window because we might miss seeing the sleigh. The cow pasture we saw through the window in the back of the house was full of trees dark against the pure snow, and the stars sparkled in the clear sky. As hard as we looked, we never did see Santa's sleigh. Every minute of kneeling by that window seemed like an hour.

Finally, finally, finally there was a loud pounding on the front door, and we raced to open it. One year I bumped my head going through the kitchen doorway. Whether a lump was forming or not, I managed to open the door. There stood Santa with a pillow case or two over his shoulder, ho ho hoing his heart out. He talked to us a little and handed out our toys and then left because he had a lot of other children to see that night.

About fifteen minutes later my father came back from the barn and couldn't believe he had missed Santa again. He was angry because he noticed that some of the cow grain and the hay was missing. It didn't take us long to figure out that reindeer get hungry, too.

We never recognized Santa's voice, his barn shoes or the pillow cases. I finally figured out that the box labeled "Red Underwear for Christmas" actually was a storage place for the professional suit my father used when he played Santa for half of South Saint Paul's youngsters before he married.

And I can hardly believe that these memories take me back more than fifty years because it just doesn't seem like that much time could have passed. But those years have passed, and the only thing that remains unchanged is the memory of how Christmas used to be when I was a kid on the farm back in Hastings. Grandma was right. Years are so much longer when you are young and waiting for Santa than they are when you are older.

Yesterday's Supermarkets
by Graham S. Frear

We are so accustomed to the vast array of foods and other products stacked in our modern supermarket cornucopias that it is difficult to imagine the typical country store of the past. My grandfather, W. S. Frear, owned two such stores west of Minneapolis from the late 1800's, and through World War I . Grandpa's first store was in Minnetonka Mills, and then he moved to Deephaven. I was not old enough to remember much about those stores, but I remember my dad talking about them.

Grandpa's stores stocked a wide range of foodstuffs, all pretty basic, in addition to items no longer found in food stores. Lighted by hanging kerosene lights and heated by a wood stove, the store was a social club with local characters exchanging news and spitting tobacco into tin cans--not always accurately.

Most country stores sold canned and bottled goods, dry goods, sewing supplies, limited hardware and tack for horses, animal feed and drugs. Vegetables and fruits in season were stocked in open bins--hardy things like carrots, beets, potatoes, turnips and squash were available most of the time because they would keep for several months in an underground space. Occasionally one would find a cabbage or rutabaga in a store, but lettuce, celery and peppers were unknown. Most people had their own kitchen gardens, and they stored dried fruits and root crops in sand. They canned vegetables and chicken in late summer and kept apples in their cellars.

Deliveries of a wide range of products were made by horse and wagon, and wholesalers supplied the stores in the same way from warehouses in Minneapolis. The driver frequently had lunch in grandmother's kitchen. As his horse munched oats from a nose bag out front, the distributor typically ate his noon meal in the kitchen of the store owner's wife. After a cold and bumpy ride in a wagon, the home cooked meal may have been one of his favorite fringe benefits. More distant suppliers sent their products by rail.

Usually items came shipped in barrels, drums, burlap bags or stout wooden boxes. Vinegar, kerosene, and molasses were dispensed from fifty-gallon barrels with spigots for dispensing into containers supplied by customers. Dried products like flour, animal feed, sugar and salt were dispensed from large bags usually stored on the floor.

Only one brand of cigarettes, Sweet Corporal, was tailor-made. All other cigarettes were rolled from papers and a bag of tobacco. Critics questioned quality control by complaining that the tobacco contained floor sweepings from the cigarette factory, but they smoked the stuff anyway. Snuff, a popular tobacco product, came in one and five pound jars and sold in oiled paper bags for five cents an ounce. Chewing tobacco came in oak boxes and was sold in four inch plugs cut from large blocks worth ten cents. Cigars were typically unwrapped and sold for five and ten cents, depending on quality.

Various crackers and cookies came in large boxes and sold by the count. Nothing came wrapped in a fancy, eye-catching package like it does today. Candies in large variety were sold in bulk from large tins and boxes. Bulk taffy, caramels, lemon drops, pink and white mints, jaw breakers, horehound drops and candies on a string sold in cutoff segments. Kids visited the store daily to buy penny candies.

Coffee came in bulk containers and paper packages, usually at eight cents a pound. Tea came in bulk boxes lined with foil. Cocoa chocolate came in paper packages. Nobody had ever heard of herbal tea, decaffeinated coffee, cocoa mix or chocolate milk.

A dairyman arrived in a horse drawn wagon to dispense fresh milk and cream. Farm-made butter came in five-pound jars or one-pound rolls. Creamery butter came in fifty-pound tubs. The store clerk dispensed butter with a wooden spatula, weighed the amount, and wrapped the order in waxed paper. Cheese, the only other dairy product, was sold from large waxed paper rounds kept under a glass dome on the counter. The clerk cut and weighed each order and wrapped it in brown paper.

Lard, which was the only shortening besides butter and pan drippings for baking and frying, was sold the same way. Five gallon empty lard tins were used to hold rice, tapioca, and dried prunes, apples, currants and raisins.

People who wanted fresh meat bought it at the butcher shop. Meat in the store was limited to products that did not require refrigeration. The store's selection consisted mainly of cured hams, bacon, and sausages that hung from hooks behind the counter. Salt pork was dispensed from large stone jars, as were dill pickles and pickled herring. Dried beef, corned beef, and roast beef came in cans, as did salmon, mackerel, and sardines. Salted dried cod and herring were available, and stores catering to Scandinavians stacked on the floor great redolent slabs of lutefisk that often provided a bed for the store's sleeping cat.

Cane sugar came in hundred pound bags and sold in bulk. Flour came in barrels.   Brown sugar often became chunky from absorbed moisture, but it was not considered spoiled. Salt, pepper, and other spices came in large tins.   Customers carried home small quantities in small paper brown bags tied with a string that came from a spool that hung overhead.

Drugs and medicines were usually patented remedies often of doubtful provenance, but Smith Brothers cough drops and Lydia Pinkam's compound for ladies were respectable household names. Cough syrups, salves, ointments, camphor, and ammonia were sold in bulk.

Baked goods were usually baked by the store owner's wife, along with bread that sold for a nickel a loaf and pies that sold for twenty cents. There were no delis in town, but the store owner's wife would sometimes make and sell ham sandwiches.

Bottled soft drinks usually included strawberry, cream soda, root beer or sasaparilla, lemon, and ginger ale--all of which sold for five cents. Apple cider was sold from barrels in the fall, and by mid-winter it had turned into the more provocative hard cider.

Cereals were limited to corn meal, oatmeal and widely popular Pettijohn's hot cereal. Later Cream of Wheat and Grapenuts came along with corn flakes and shredded wheat. Rice was sold in bulk from large white cloth bags.

Of course, food stored and shipped in this manner contained some rodent droppings, weevils, flour moths and other contaminants modern shoppers would consider unacceptable.   The accepted practice was to take the food home, wash it, and hope the heat from cooking would kill anything that might hurt us.   Recycling was a way of life.   Customers supplied bottles, cans, tins, boxes and crocks.   Whatever inconvenience this caused was considered necessary.

Eidam Frear store on Minnetonka Boulevard in Minnetonka Mills, 1890

My grandpa sold products that we wouldn't think of looking for in today's grocery store.   One could buy buggy whips, harness fastenings and leather strapping for harness repair, axle grease and livestock salt in large cakes.   Hardware like screws, screening, rivets, fencing and staples were part of the inventory.   He also sold hand drills, leather punches, screwdrivers, planes and hand drills.

Grandpa's store was redolent of kerosene, slab bacon, cheese, bulk coffee, molasses, apples in barrels and axle grease.   Contrast this with the lack of aromas in today's supermarkets.   Today we are spoiled by a wealth of exotic foods in exotic wrappings.   Consumers get whatever they want whenever they want it.   We get grapes from Chile and apples from Mexico. Tomatoes, melons, berries and bananas are available year round because they are shipped from Mexico, Spain and Central America.

Before I was old enough to hang around the store, my grandfather sold it and retired.   From his home nearby, he'd give me money after dinner and send me over to the store to buy him a beer from the new owner.   Since my dad was a teetotaler, I considered it quite an adventure when Grandpa would fill the bottle cap with beer and let me take a sip.

My grandfather would be bewildered by the vast array of frozen and processed foods that line the aisles of today's supermarkets.   He wouldn't know what to make of Tombstone Pizza and Chinese vegetables, arugula and Ranch dressing, Haagen Daz ice cream and Crest toothpaste. He would be amazed to see these products, and if he saw the prices, he would be really amazed.

Graham S. Frear graduated from St. Olaf after interrupting his studies to serve in the U. S. Marine Corps in World War II. He taught English at Northfield High School and was president of the Minnesota Council of Teachers of English before becoming an Irish scholar and English Professor Emeritus at St. Olaf College in Northfield.

Fighting for Causes
by Graham S. Frear

My grandmother, Clara Chase Frear, a store owner's wife in Minnetonka Mills, was an inveterate writer of letters, supporter of causes and advocate of many social concerns and organizations. She wrote hundreds of letters to people she knew, a weekly column for the local county newspaper, and letters to the editor and to a wide range of public figures.

She was a member of the Anti-saloon League, the Women's Christian Temperance Union, the First Church of Christian Scientist since its conception, the Women's Missionary Society, the Anti-vivisection Society, the Humane Society, and the Grand Army of the Republic as a surviving daughter of a captain killed in the Civil War. She espoused women's suffrage and better treatment of women in the workplace.

Grandmother kept voluminous scrapbooks of significant news stories, obituaries of famous people (I recall Tennyson and Whitman among them), playbills from Twin Cities theaters and opera houses, picture postcards and trading cards.

I remember her sitting at her dining room table, by the window, in her chair equipped with rollers because she couldn't walk well. The table was covered with letters, correspondence ready to mail, clippings, and recent newspapers. She was a one-woman crusade for a wide range of causes, most positive but some not. She was a feminist before it became popular, a worker for women's rights in politics, the workplace, and in the home. My grandfather was either a man who paid little attention to all this or the most tolerant of human beings. I suspect the latter because their marriage was a long and happy one. I have some of his love letters written to her as they were about to become engaged.

It is ironic that I have absolutely no copies of anything she ever wrote. The only thing I have is a letter she received in 1927 from the Anti-Compulsory Vaccination Committee in New York. Receivers of this letter were encouraged to arrange personal interviews with their representatives to join the fight against Senator Kennedy's bill that would require school children to be vaccinated. Although smallpox, pertussis, and diptheria had taken a heavy toll of life throughout the world, the development of vaccines since the 18th century had not been entirely successful. In some cases, the rate of deaths among vaccinated children was higher than the death rate of those who contracted the disease. Many people did not trust the new vaccines. As a Christian Scientist, my grandmother opposed government action that would force parents to take such a risk.

It is difficult for me to determine in these modern times when we have seen the eradication of diptheria, smallpox and polio through vaccination, whether my grandmother's concerns were well-founded in 1927. That my dear grandmother directed her energies to this cause, however, continues to amaze me. She possessed strong beliefs and she was willing to fight for her causes.

Clara Chase Frear and Walter Scott Frear in the front seat, their daughter Aureline Frear (right) and a friend in the back, circa 1907.

Lady and Babe
by Alice Stielow

Our family moved to a farm near Graceville in 1936, and what a great place it was with a big house, big barn, and running water. While my older sister Dolores spent most of her time working in the house, my younger sister Francie and I enjoyed all the outdoor activities and adventures that a farm could offer a couple of little girls.

Lady and Babe were our work horses that we used to do chores when we needed to pull heavy loads. They were used for everything from hauling hay to raking hay or pulling the manure spreader into the barn to be loaded and then to the fields to spread the fertilizer over the fields. They were a pretty docile team that could be trusted to stand for a long time while loading or unloading. Because Babe was high-spirited, she would throw her head back and lay her ears flat when she didn't think things were going her way. Lady was more patient, but as a team they worked well together.

Francie and I asked Daddy many times if we could ride Babe and Lady, but the answer was always no. Those horses were for working. With logic and bravado typical for 8 and 10-year-old children, we thought, "Okay, they are work horses, but who says we can't try to ride them when no one is looking?"

One great summer day, Daddy and Mother were gone somewhere. Since they had told us to do chores, we knew they would be late. The opportunity we had waited for was at hand, and those horses looked so inviting. We decided that we would only try one at a time.

Because Lady was more docile, we decided to start with her. However, when we brought her to the gate on the west side of the barn and began to prepare her for riding, she wasn't her usual docile self. When we tried to get the bridle on her, she threw her head in the air and refused the bit, the piece of smooth round metal that goes in the horse's mouth on top of the tongue. The bridle consists of leather straps that go over the ears and around the neck, and then buckle on the side of the head; the bit connects to the straps. When you put a bridle on a horse, the bit goes in the mouth first and then the straps are slipped over the ears and neck.

Lady wasn't used to kids doing this, and I am sure we didn't do it the same as Mother or Daddy did, but after several tries, we got a little better at getting it in her mouth right, and she stopped throwing her head in the air. She finally decided two dumb kids were going to get the job done one way or the other. We had watched adults put a bridle on a horse many times, and back in the late 30's, kids helped out all over the farm when needed, so we weren't afraid to try most anything.

Finally, Lady took the bit, and we slipped the leather straps over her ears and around her neck. Boy, we thought we had accomplished a great feat. I guess we really had.

Hey, after all that, who gets to ride first? Francie crawled up on the gate to try to mount Lady. We were to ride bareback because a saddle was something that didn't live at our place. After several tries, with Lady always getting as far away from the gate as possible, we realized we had to come up with a better plan.

As we were figuring new strategy, Lady stepped on my foot, scraping all the skin off the top, and blood ran down onto my toes. Naturally I screamed in pain, but determination to ride Lady was our only concern, and we had to hurry because time was going fast. The new plan was that I would coax Lady with some oats to take her mind off someone getting on her back. Okay, that sounded like a great idea. All the time we wondered just how much time we would have before we had to start chores or--worse yet--before Mother and Daddy came home and caught us.

I grabbed a pail, tore off to the granary, and brought back some oats, leaving a trail of blood in both directions. As soon as I returned with the oats, Lady stuck her nose in the pail. Seizing the opportunity we had waited for, Francie jumped on Lady's back, holding onto her mane and the bridle straps for dear life.

Lady took off across the yard in a jump and a fast run. If only Francie had been toting a gun, one would have thought she was Annie Oakley riding around the yard. I stood there with my mouth open and wondered if Lady would stop when she got to the barn. I quickly closed the barn door, and when she got there she just stopped and stood there, as if she had always had someone sitting on her back.

Okay for the horse, but Francie's eyes were still as large as saucers as she slid to the ground and asked if I wanted a turn. Now call me chicken or call me anything, but I wasn't about to get on Lady until I had gone to the house to soak my foot in some good hot water and bandage it. So we put Lady back in the pasture for that day. We couldn't wait for Mother and Daddy to leave us home again so we could resume horseback riding.

I hobbled back to the house to attend to my foot, which was really hurting by now because all the excitement was over for the time being. After I soaked it for awhile, Francie got peroxide and we poured that over it, then got out the Raleigh's cow salve and covered it. Finally we found a piece of sheet to wrap around it. That done, we decided it was time to start chores, but first we had to make up a story about how I got hurt. Well, maybe George Washington couldn't tell a lie when he chopped down the cherry tree, but we had to think of something fast, and we had to make sure we both told the same story. WE decided to say that I fell and got my foot caught between two gates when we started doing the chores. That sounded pretty believable-- like it really could have happened. Okay, now that was settled.

We raced off to the barn, me with a nice white wrapped foot, which would only stay white for a few minuets. Francie felt sorry for me and wanted me to stay out of the manure and mud. Well, that didn't sound too bad, so while she put in the cows, I carried feed. She took the feed into the barn and emptied the pails while I came with the next pails full. It was about that time when Daddy came to the barn. When he saw me limping across the barnyard, he noticed my bandaged foot and wanted to know what had happened. Well, I told my story and he seemed to believe what I said. Okay, got by that one.

When Mother soon arrived with the milk pails, she too wanted to know what had happened, but she asked Francie. Boy, we were lucky we had gotten our story straight before our parents came home.

Mother sat down and started milking, and when Francie came by, she asked her again. I guess she wasn't quite as gullible as daddy had been. She called me to come and show her how bad it was. I grabbed a milk stool, sat down and unwrapped the now dragging-behind bandage from my foot. All she said was. " Get out of the barn, and go to the house."

Now that didn't sound too bad either, but then Mother said I had to help Dolores get supper and set the table. Shoot, I thought I was going to get out of some work.

Chores done, supper over, I hated to admit how bad the darn foot was throbbing, but finally I told Mother, and she couldn't imagine how I could fall and get my foot caught in the gates. Oh well, I had to soak it again in Lysol water and then she put raw salt pork on it and wrapped it up for the night. Not wanting to let the cat out of the bag, I suffered through the night and several days until it got better and I could quit limping around. Salt pork was the cure-all when we got hurt or stepped on a nail. It would draw out the poison we were told, and it must have because when you removed the bandage each morning, it would be just green and full of matter.

Days passed, and we waited for another opportunity to ride Lady. Finally we got brave and took her out behind the barn where no one could see us, and this time she was really good and let us put the bridle on as we stood on the feed pails to be able to reach her. We pretty much just stayed behind the barn and rode her around and around, each taking turns. We waited for another opportunity to see if Babe would cooperate and let us ride her too, and we soon got a chance. Our parents said they were going to Alexandria to see a doctor. Waiting was almost too much for us two little ragamuffins, but wait we did, and then the big day came when our parents would be gone for several hours. Off we raced to the barn to get our horses.

Babe must have thought it was working time as she let us put the bridle on without any trouble, and Lady gave us no trouble. Great! Now we could each have a horse. I got on Lady, and Francie got on Babe. Babe decided to do a little barn dance when Francie got on, but she soon settled down when she saw Lady go out the door. GREAT JUMPIN JEHOVE! We were both on horses and really riding.

Now what could happen? Only the worst. Dolores saw us out there on the horses, and she was going to tell Mother and Daddy about it if we didn't come in and help her with the housework. We had to get her to swear to keep our secret until the horses really were letting us ride with ease. Then we were going to SHOW Mother and Daddy that we had accomplished the impossible. So we helped Dolores the rest of the afternoon, just to keep her quiet.

A couple weeks later we told Daddy that we had ridden the horses, and he said, " I knew you were up to something." After that we rode and got the cows in the pasture every day. Sometimes the horses were in the pasture too, and we tried catching them and riding them home, but it took quite a while until we were big enough to do that.

Lady and Babe gave us many hours of riding fun-- even if they were work horses that we were not supposed to ride. We didn't care. They were our best friends.

Alice Stielow and her husband Richard have lived on the same farm near Clinton for 54 years. They have 5 daughters, 1 son, 22 grandchildren and 20 great grandchildren, and they had several foster children. Alice worked with physically and mentally handicapped people for 31 years.

Things My Grandmother Told Me
by Patricia Ryan

My mother, Claire Leverty Ryan, was a teacher, and my father, Bill Ryan, built houses. I was born near South St. Paul between Highway 56 and Inver Grove Trail. With both parents working, I spent much time with my grandmother, Ann Borden Ryan, who told me story after story about the old times.

My grandmother was tall, about five feet seven inches and of medium build. She wore glasses, but her blue eyes were intense. When she was in her twenties, cataracts nearly blinded her. She had surgery in her thirties, and I remember putting drops in her eyes when she was older. I remember being a little child and listening so intently to my grandmother's tales of the earlier times--of our ancestors. My great great grandfather Borden had come from Slyne Head in the mid 1850's. When my grandmother's mother died in Vally Conneely in County Galway, Ireland, my great grandfather sold his place there and came to Minnesota.

My grandmother said that her father, Patrick Borden, bought land in 1866, when she was just a year old, on what is now the Inver Grove Trail. He paid just $15 per acre and cut the wood to clear the land. The wood was piled up beside the river to be transported and sold in St. Paul.

When winter came and the river froze, the men of the area who were all selling their wood, made big sledges from the trees and hauled wood by oxen to St. Paul. A man would walk ahead of the teams with an ax sounding the ice for thickness. Only once was a team of oxen lost. As my grandfather got money for the wood, he would add more land. When he could afford it, he would replace the oxen with horses.

In 1887, my grandmother Ann Borden married John Ryan, who lived near where Sibley High School is today. They built a house and barn and settled down to raise their two sons. There was no mail delivery at that time, so once a week my grandmother rode her horse to pick up the mail at Pine Bend, where the monument is on the highway today.

When my dad was little, he and his father and the other area men used to cut big hunks of ice out of Pratt's lake, near the junction of Inver

Grove Trail and highways 52, 55 and 56. They sold the ice to ice dealers in St. Paul who stored the ice in sawdust so it could be used to keep food cold and safe in ice boxes.

My father also shot timber wolves for extra income. There were many wolves in the area at that time, and hunters were paid $20 per wolf. My grandmother said they had to take one ear to Hastings for the bounty. I can't remember if it was the right ear or left ear, but it was always the same side ear to be sure no one was paid twice for the same wolf. My grandmother said that the last wolf she saw was in the 1920's when it came to drink at the pond behind her house. In the 1940's a single pair of wolves were seen down by the Spring Lake. There are lots of coyotes in that area today, but no more wolves.

My beloved grandmother died in 1950, my father died in 1951, and my mother died in 1980 in Tucson. I moved back to the old Minnesota neighborhood where I grew up, but the place is not the same. Our area in Inver Grove Heights is building up at a tremendous pace. I really hate to see it because it's so crowded, and it doesn't have the same beautiful spirit as it had when I was a kid. But the memories are wonderful. On quiet nights I can still hear my grandmother telling stories about oxen hauling logs over the frozen water, about harvesting ice, and about the howling timber wolves I remember, too, the blue of my Grandmother Ann Ryan Borden's eyes.

John and Mary Borden Ryan

Patricia Ryan taught elementary school in South St. Paul and Tucson. She lives in South St. Paul, where she is a companion for Catholic Charities.

Thanks, Mom!
by Jon Lynott

My mom, Mary Lindbeck Lynott, was a world class worrier, but she came by it honestly – her mother had honed worrying to a fine art, and Grandma probably got it from her mother.

I have vivid memories of Grandma pacing the floor at the family cabin near Ely, in a scene repeated every summer weekend of my childhood. Grandpa had been tramping through his woods since lunch. Grandma wanted to go home to start dinner, but Grandpa, who loved his piece of God's country on Little Long Lake, was reluctant to leave.

As if it would hurry him along, she would lean out the door and yell, "Fritz...FRIIIIIIIITZ!" in her high, thin voice. Nobody had the heart to tell her that she could scarcely be heard from the other side of the room. Later though, I came to understand that Grandma wasn't yelling for his benefit, but for her own. She kept herself busy with this trivial task to avoid the image of some bear having eaten her husband for dinner.

Isn't it the American way for each generation to try to improve on the ways of the past? Well, instead of Grandma's pacing and hand wringing, Mom's style of worry was more refined and subtle. She showed few outward signs of distress. She was always busy with chores and duties of a wife and mother. But when she was anxious, she went into overdrive with extra baking and sewing and cleaning to mask her concern. In fact, many times we never knew she was worried until the crisis passed and she would relax. Only then would she talk about the weird "what if" scenarios, the macabre photoplay that tormented her imagination, and how the nearly constant prayer kept her private terror at bay.

And when I look back on it, I guess we gave her plenty to worry about. She herded eight active kids through the terrible twos into the troubled teenage years and beyond over the course of a couple decades. Guiding eight young souls to be God-fearing adults while making a home and being a loving wife was plenty of work. Add to that being active in the community and re-establishing a career when the last of us started school. She knew stress before the term was trendy!

Mom would worry at the drop of a hat. To assuage her fears (her unfounded fears, mind you), I would occasionally engage in the white lie. It was for her own good, you understand. "No sense in worrying about nothing," I would rationalize. "Why have her wringing her hands over details that she'll never need to know about? Better to let her sleep well thinking that everything is fine," I thought--especially since everything really *was* fine. I was a responsible person. Well… reasonably responsible. I got into a few scrapes, but I was not one to be brash or to take needless risks.

Eventually we all grew up and left our Duluth east side home to take on the world and make our place in it. But she was still mothering, across the miles that separated us. She kept in touch and wanted to know about our challenges and victories. She was ever ready to dispense motherly support and advice and to cheer us on our way. I could move hundreds of miles away, establish myself in my adopted hometown, become proficient in my career, marry and start a family, be active in my community--but I was still her little boy!

About fifteen years ago, I was arranging a trip with my young son Phil. A weekend air show back home in Duluth would be a perfect father-son getaway. I called Mom to see if we could stay with her and Dad. "Of course, you're welcome to stay here," she told me, "but we will be out of town." We started chatting about arrangements and the air show and the other things going on in her life and mine. She stopped abruptly in mid sentence, paused a few seconds, then asked apprehensively, "You're not bringing Phil up here on your motorcycle, are you?"

I swallowed hard. One of the more attractive features of this road trip was traveling by motorcycle. I had plenty of experience commuting to and from work. I'd made several day-trips and overnight trips with my wife, always in complete safety, usually in relative comfort, and enjoying every mile of the experience. Phil knew the safety rules well because I drilled them into him every time we rode together. I deliberated on the fact that they wouldn't be home and would never find out. I lied.

She sounded relieved and gave voice to the feeling. "Good," she replied as she let out the breath she was holding. I correctly guessed that the image of us traveling by motorcycle was triggering anxiety that would be full-fledged worry in no time, and the air show was still weeks away. She went on to explain, "I wouldn't want to have to worry about...," when she stopped again. After another pause she queried, "Are you telling the truth?"

I swallowed hard again. "No," I admitted.

What followed was my explanation that I was a safe driver and that Phil was a good passenger and traveling companion. That was followed by plenty of examples of times we had ridden together safely, the thousands of miles I'd ridden without so much as a scratch, and her not buying a word of it. But she relinquished the decision to me when she said, "I'll be praying overtime that weekend."

"Thanks, Mom," I returned, "I can always use prayers."

Phil and I enjoyed a great weekend--the weather, the sights, sounds, smells, and the male bonding. The air show was exciting, and touring my son around my old hometown was a special delight. Heck, just the ride there and back was fun, and it enriched both of us to share the experience. The whole weekend turned into another fabulous memory added to the treasury that is ours.

We returned home Sunday night safe and sound, though maybe a little road weary. Because we hadn't a single mishap, I told my wife that Mom's worrying and prayers were wasted. As I drifted off to sleep that night though, I changed my mind. Maybe the weekend was a smashing success because of the fervent prayers of this mother and grandmother.

Mom found that sharing burdens with God made them a little lighter and that sharing joys made them more glorious. Her example helped me to see that saving my communication with God for life and death situations was short sighted. It led me to make mini-prayers all day long, thanking God for sunrises and safe commutes, and asking for strength to face life's challenges and problems.

I've come to think about that incident more and more lately. After all, it's a topsy-turvy world out there that can be so strange at times. My babies have grown and left the nest to make their mark on the world. Will they be happy, fruitful, successful? Have I prepared them for life? Can they deal with adversity? So many crazy, weird possibilities out there can give a parent plenty to worry about.

But then, I come by my tendency to worry honestly. I inherited it. And thanks, Mom!

Jon Lynott and his mom, Mary Lindbeck Lynott, Leaving Holy Rosary Church in Duluth approximately forty years ago.

Jon Lynott graduated from Duluth East High School. He lives in Mound with Sue, the woman of his dreams, and he tries not to worry too much about his children Phil and Betsey. He describes himself as a reluctant metro-lander who is an Iron Ranger by birth and a Duluth kid at heart.

Taming an Ornery Calf
by Ed Putzier

A major activity for farm kids was the 4-H club. The club met once a month, rotating among homes of members' parents. The meetings always opened with the Pledge of Allegiance, followed by the 4-H pledge: "I pledge my Head to clearer thinking, my Heart to greater loyalty, my Hands to larger service, and my Health to better living." After a business meeting, refreshments were served and games of some sort prevailed.

Shortly after the first of each year, a member had to select a project to complete by the third week in August for the county 4-H fair held in Central Park of nearby Litchfield. Both boys and girls showed animals-- pigs, dairy calves, beef calves, sheep, colts, a pen of turkeys, ducks, geese, or chickens. Records of feed consumption and other activities associated with raising an animal were part of the requirements. Many of the girls' projects were related to baking, sewing, or other home crafts.

I was a junior in high school when I decided to show a Holstein heifer calf. With Pa's help, I selected Daisy. Born in September of the previous year, Daisy would grow to about 500 pounds by fair time. Keeping track of feed consumption and daily activities was no problem. In April I put a halter on Daisy and took her outside to begin teaching her to lead and assume a show-ring stance, something she would have to do for a judge at fair time. Right from the start, Daisy gave me nothing but trouble. She led me more than I led her.

Fair day arrived. As we sat at breakfast, I didn't mention it and hoped Pa and Ma didn't remember. I ate fast, left the table, and went out to service the tractor and plow, hoping I'd get to the field before anyone realized what day it was. I had no more than started when Pa came out the door. "Aren't you supposed to take your calf to the fair today?" he said.

I responded, "She's too ornery. I can't handle her."

Pa replied, "You take her in and make the best of it." We never argued with Pa.

With considerable effort, Ma and I loaded Daisy in the horse trailer. We got to town, unloaded her, and tied her to the stanchion. With brush and curry comb, I did some last-minute grooming and soon heard the call to the show ring for Holstein heifers. With a great deal of tugging, Daisy entered the ring, along with a dozen or so other calves. Daisy had to walk for the judge and stand in a spread stance while he gave her the once-over. It wasn't easy to control her.

All of a sudden, the judge directed me to take Daisy to one side of the ring. He then selected another to stand beside us, and then another, and so on. He lined us all up and came over to where Daisy and I were and announced I had the blue ribbon calf. I couldn't believe it. We left the ring but had to get ready for the parade. I was told I would lead the Holstein group with other calves following four abreast. I had visions of Daisy crashing into store windows and Pa being sued for allowing such a wild animal in town.

After a couple of blocks of strenuous tugging with a firm grip on the halter, Daisy started to behave. Perhaps she realized she was somewhat of a celebrity. By the time we were on the street to head back to the park, she was leading like an old cow.

After we returned to the park, it was time for showing the Grand Championship of all breeds-- Ayrshires, Guernseys, Jerseys, Brown Swiss, as well as my Holstein. Daisy and I had to enter the ring again. This time she did everything I asked her to do. Again the judge sent us to the side of the ring. We had won the Grand Championship!

Pa didn't say much when we got home, but he had that look in his eye--he was right again. Daisy remained on the farm, and a year and a half later entered her life of cowhood. I suppose, as she grazed in the pasture, her comment to the other cows might have been, "Girls, you should have seen me when I was a calf."

Ed Putzier grew up near Litchfield. After graduating from Mankato State, he earned an advanced degree in physics at the University of Rochester in New York. He worked at Rocky Flats Nuclear Weapons plant in Colorado.

PTA Meetings
by Ed Putzier

It seemed that everyone in the school district, including the kids, grandparents, and parents, attended PTA meetings--a major social event for farm families. Our school was located in the little village of Greenleaf, just two miles from the farm. Grandpa and Grandma Stenberg lived just a block from the school.

An hour or so before the meeting, Grandpa walked to the schoolhouse to fuel, pressurize, and light the Coleman lanterns and hang them from the ceiling. While he was working on the lights, Grandma was busy starting coffee. She mixed about twelve eggs (to settle the grounds) with ground coffee and added the mixture to the water in three large granite coffee pots. A three-burner kerosene stove provided heat for boiling the coffee.

The business meeting was usually quite short because there were never any earth-shaking items to talk about. Participation by the teacher was very minimal. Everyone was more interested in the program and lunch that followed.

Local talent, including vocal and instrumental musicians, frequently performed. At least once a year, Mrs. Goemer, with her slow and wide-range vibrato, sang, "I wandered today through the hills, Maggie." John and Thea Olson, with daughter Margaret, also sang. John strummed his guitar and with Swedish accent, the trio sang, "Darling I am growing old-- silver threads among the gold."

As we grew older, my brother Sid and I were frequently asked to play polka, waltz, and schottische music for the program. I played accordion and Sid played violin. I recall four male high school teachers who sang excellent four-part harmony. It was always a treat to hear from them.

Billy Waller--bachelor farmer, craftsman, violin maker, and violinist--was an accomplished musician. Unfortunately, no one in the community played piano well enough to be his accompanist. Billy made his violin sing, and his repertoire included some of the well-known Kreisler compositions.

We kids were always bored with speakers and considered it a disappointment if they comprised the evening's program. From time to time, someone told about his travels. A priest or minister always seemed willing to speak. The county agent would sometimes be requested to talk about recent developments in farming. The adults seemed interested, but the kids felt short changed.

After the PTA business meeting and entertainment, it was time for lunch. There were sandwiches of various sorts, pickles, cookies, cake, Jello, and Grandma's coffee. We kids had to be satisfied with water because there was no pop or lemonade. Ladies talked homemaking, and men talked farming. Very little relating to education was ever talked about. It seemed everyone was always satisfied that the teacher was providing us with a good education. As I think back, I believe that was a correct assumption.

Farm Kids and Animals
by Betty Jean Rueckert Collins

I grew up in Minnesota Lake, the world capital of nicknames. George "Yatz" Bach and his family were our neighbors, and his kids were my playmates. In observance of local custom, Yatz made sure we all had nicknames. Yatz's kids were called "Stupe," "Gangleshanks," "Tubby" and "Punky," and my sister and I were "Jelly Bean" and "Stinker." As farm kids, we had to do our share of chores, but we also had a lot of fun, and most of our play involved our love of all the animals that were such an important part of our daily lives.

Ma thought I would never learn to walk because I was convinced I was meant to be a horse. Most of the time I acted out the role by clip clopping on all fours, clutching wooden blocks with my hands to produce hoof sounds. Our linoleum floors helped perfect that sound effect. Colored aluminum popcorn bowls, arranged in a row on our bottom stair step, made my feed trough manger. Sometimes I put a string in my mouth for a reins as my little sister rode on my back.

Outside my sister and I transformed our horse play to the upright position, complete with favorite old broomstick front legs. We galloped everywhere. Pa made us tin heads for more broomstick horses that we galloped across the door yard.

When Gangleshanks and Tubby came over to play, they added their own creative details to the game. Both used tree branches to make stick horses. Gangleshanks completely stripped the bark to make a palomino, and she stripped it intermittently for a pinto effect. We wrapped twine around trees in the groves of both our farms to create make-believe ranches. Heaven protect any stranger who accidentally might wander into our territory.

Paper dolls just didn't cut it with us horse lovers; we preferred paper horses. Gangleshanks, Tubby, Stinker and I spent many days drawing horses, coloring and cutting them out. We'd see how individual we could create our horses and then exchange with each other the way other kids traded comic books.

Real horses became part of our lives. We all had ponies. Diamond and Midnight were the first of several horses that have been a part of my life. Thunder belonged to the Bach kids. Town kids frequently came out to play with us and ride our ponies.

Shaggy the donkey was another favorite family pet. Shaggy kept the cows in line. When the cows were inside the barn, Shaggy stood outside and called them out. After a series of hee-haws, the cows stampeded out of the barn. If the cows were outside, Shaggy went into the barn and the stampede went the other direction. Once Shaggy got away and wandered over to the neighbors' farm, where he recreated the same scenario with their cows.

One spring day I was riding Shaggy along the lane when a pheasant flew up and surprised both of us. Shaggy stopped abruptly, but I kept right on going--into the mud.

Not all my mud experiences involved Shaggy. One of the craziest adventures happened when Tubby and I decided to pretend we were pigs. A low spot on the trail between our two places would turn into a giant mud puddle after a rain. We knew that pigs wallowed in mud to keep cool, so why not us?

Our first step into the mud was the hardest, but after things got started, we finally took the big plunge and got down on our hands and knees. Finally we lay down up to our necks in mud. It sure was fun while it lasted, but what were we to do when it was time to go home? Big decision--your place or mine for the clean-up?

Since it was a little closer to Tubby's house, that is where we headed. When she came to the door, I asked, "Mrs. Bach, can we take a bath?" She took one look at us, sent me home, and tried to give her daughter a spanking. She got so muddy that she had to give up on that.

When I reached home, I stood at the basement door and called, "Ma, I'm dirty as a pig." She sent me to the hydrant by the pig pens for clean-up, pronto.

Most of our farm games were not as messy as that, but some were just as crazy. Stinker and I had an old metal bed with a wide-spaced bar headboard. We'd pull the bed away from the wall, kneel on the mattress, and then stick our heads through the stanchion bars and pretend we were cows.

And my memories of growing up on the farm wouldn't be complete without the cats, dogs, baby calves, and other farm animals as companions. Growing up in those times, with parents who went through the Great Depression, our work and play experiences with those farm animals gave us an appreciation and understanding of life, consequences and loss.

Eventually we went back to our legal names. Barb, Maxine and I went on to be nurses. My sister Janet majored in Spanish and history at the University of Wyoming and settled down in Albuquerque. Maxine and I returned to work and live on our family farms where it all began so many wears ago. We sometimes get together and talk about those good old days.

Gangleshanks and Thunder

Betty Jean Collins retired from nursing at the Mapleton Community Home, and her husband retired from farming. They live in Wells and spend winters in Apache Junction, Arizona. They have two adult daughters.

Depression Years at the Packing House
by Mary Bongard

As much as we wanted jobs, we just couldn't find jobs. My husband and I had two sons born in 1928 and 1929, and right after they were born, the stock market crash signaled the end of the Roaring Twenties and the beginning of the Great Depression

Without jobs, it was almost impossible to afford even life's necessities, though prices were in line with wages during the 1930's. Bread was eight cents a loaf, eggs were about twenty cents a dozen, a half pound of bacon was forty cents, flour and sugar cost less than a nickel a pound, and gas cost fifteen cents a gallon.

Glewwe's Grocery Store in South St. Paul deserves so much praise and thanks from so many people, including my family. They allowed us to charge everyday groceries such as milk and bread. We purchased everything on credit and paid when we could. There was no money exchanged at the time of purchase. Glewwe's helped so many people have food, and they never sent a bill or charged interest to any of us.

We moved around a lot--lived with my parents and with my husband's parents. It wasn't easy living with family when the kids were little so we moved to various cheap apartments with our two little kids. Our rent was eight dollars a month. This seems low today, but in the 1930's, it was difficult to pay for anything.

During the 1930's there were no jobs. My husband worked a pick and shovel as part of a WPA job. The Works Progress Administration was a government program during the Depression that enabled people to have jobs that paid a very small amount so they wouldn't starve. WPA workers completed many projects designed to improve public spaces, such as sidewalks, retaining walls, parks and roads. The jobs paid a few dollars a week, and when one project was completed, the workers had to look for something else to build. You can still see W PA stamped on old sidewalks and structures at places like Como Park and Minnehaha Falls. What you need to remember is that building those structures kept many of us alive during those years.

We managed somehow with my husband's WPA salary for several months. Then a wonderful thing happened. I was able to get a job, and that same year my husband was able to find a job--both at the Armour Meat Packing Plant in South St. Paul. I was hired for seventeen cents an hour six days a week in the sausage department.

Meat packing and slaughter houses were the main industry in South St. Paul, the home of the largest stockyard in the world, and five meat packing companies eventually provided jobs for thousands of workers. Swift and Company was already up and running when the Armour plant opened in 1919. When some jobs became available, we were happy to take them. We workers were a mixture of types--black and white, young and old, men and women.

My work in the sausage department involved one man stuffing the meat into the casings fast enough to keep three women working on the finish work with the sausages. Finish work was mainly tying off sausages weighing them, and making sure they had the right length. It was slow work, all hand work. Everything had to be measured. Machines came in later, and one man on a machine stuffer kept two women working. That was piece work. You were paid for the number of sausages you completed

I hired a number of babysitters who worked cheap, just to have some money coming in. As time went on, our wages went up to twenty five cents an hour, and we continued to work six days a week. Later on, we went on piece work five days a week. This was much better-- so much better. I was able to buy groceries with some earnings and each week pay Glewwes on the huge bill we owed. It took me a long three years to get squared with Glewwes. I thanked those people over and over.

The Armour Packinghouse in South St. Paul was the most modern of meat factories--it was told to us. According to the newspaper, about 2,100 people worked at Armours during that time.

Our department was cold because the meat had to be kept cold. We wore sweaters under our Armour frocks and light weight boots to protect ourselves from floors that were always wet and slippery. Under our boots we wore wool stockings to keep our feet warm, but it didn't do much good; we were cold all the time.

When we weren't cold we were hot. In the summer and in the heat of the afternoon, parts of the plant were like walking into an oven. And my hard day's work didn't end when I left the job because I had to walk home for years until bus service started.

In 1939 my uncle died and we bought his house, a former school house on a corner lot at 13th Avenue in South St. Paul. We put $15 down and paid $15 a month for the house that cost $1500. Whenever we could afford it, we fixed it up and added on until it was a pretty nice place.

When times got better, I went to a store and picked out a beautiful silk dress--something I had dreamed of owning for many years. I put a little bit of money down and put the dress on layaway. After I made several small payments, the dress was finally mine. Although that dress might not be considered a treasure by some people's standards, it symbolized a reward for many years of hard work and sacrifice.

I retired in 1969. The Armour plant closed ten years later as a new plant was getting ready to hire people in another state. I am now 96 years old so I've seen a lot. I've seen some tough times. Surviving those tough times makes the good times seem even better.

Mary Bongard lives in Livermore, California, where she has lived since 1978. She is most proud of her two sons, who became flight engineers. They are now both retired. She has five grandchildren and eleven great-grandchildren--seven of whom are in college.

We Made the Right Move
by Carol Adair Brune

I was born and raised in Albert Lea, about as far south in Minnesota as one can get. I now find myself living in Baudette, on the Canadian border. I laugh when I hear people refer to Brainerd and Bemidji as "up north," because from my perspective those towns are in the middle of the state. We live more than a hundred miles north of Bemidji.

How did I get up here? First I married a farmer--something I never planned to do. When we started going out, neighbors were suspicious when Arlen picked me up for a date at 9 p.m. But before we could go out, he always had to bale hay and milk cows. Often on weekends he'd pick me up at 4 p.m., and I'd change my nurse's uniform and go out to the farm and help him milk cows before our evening date.

Because of all his farm responsibilities, we had a difficult time setting a wedding date. We were married on January 31, 1969, a very cold and snowy evening. That afternoon we had attended the funeral of a friend killed in Viet Nam. We went to Austin, a few miles away, for our honeymoon while Arlen's brother-in-law, a farm agent, milked the cows for his first and last time.

Although I was a city girl, I soon learned to drive tractor and rake and bale hay. We had four children, and our oldest daughter Cheryl was almost born in the barn. I brought her out there in a buggy while we milked cows, and she soon began feeding calves and playing with various cats and her dog. Four years later Linda joined the party, and fifteen months later our twins Dale and Deb showed up. We certainly had our hands full, and all the kids lived farm life to the fullest.

We lived near Albert Lea, and farming in southern Minnesota was good, but my husband was allergic to corn pollen and ragweed, which were abundant in that area. From the first year of our marriage we looked for a place to buy up north, and in 1972 we traveled to Baudette and looked at a farm. We liked it, but the owners decided not to sell. Over the years we almost bought other places in Bemidji, but in 1983 the owners of the Baudette place called and told us that they wanted to sell their place to us.

I grew up in the same Albert Lea house my mother grew up in, so moving far away was a wrenching experience. Our children had school friends, we both had family, and our network of farm friends with whom we shared good times and bad meant a lot to us. We had an infant son buried in the church cemetery there, so it was difficult to move to Baudette.

The entire process of moving our farm equipment and livestock took almost a year to complete. We had given the previous owners a lifetime lease on the house so we needed to find a place to live and get the land ready. Arlen moved a tractor and some equipment and came up in the fall to work the land. That left me and four children in Albert Lea for awhile. We moved farm equipment and furniture nearly 500 miles with our pick-up and trailer. In one load a bed was under the manure spreader.

When the family moved in May, my husband and son rode in the truck with a load on the trailer that included one dog and eleven cats, and I followed with the van, three daughters, Grandma, and boxes of African violets. With our big loads, we weren't always sure we could make it under the overpasses.

When the time came to bring up the last load, Arlen went back with the truck and trailer and was bringing his mother back also when disaster struck. Because of a flat tire on the fifth wheel, they had to pull off I35 near Clarks Grove. As they pulled back on, they were pushed off the road by one semi and another semi hit them with a load that included 100 gallon drums of paint. Nobody was seriously hurt, but a big hole was burned in the road, the truck was totaled, and Arlen and his mother returned to Baudette by car.

The first year, we lived in town and farmed five miles away. I got a job as a home care nurse--just until my husband got on his feet. I still have that job. We rented out our Albert Lea farm just in case the kids didn't like life in the far north.

By our second Christmas, we cut down a Christmas tree and moved into our new double wide on the farm. We had bricks for steps, but it was home, and it was new. The kids enjoyed living in the country again, even though they needed rides to school and social activities. Cheryl was able to get her farm permit and do some of the driving.

The kids had many opportunities they may not have had in a larger town. They became active in 4-H, which was a very close group. They went to the state fair yearly, and took trips to Washington, D.C. and Quebec. They had chances to participate in sports and other school activities, and they made many good friends. They really enjoyed life in Baudette, even though it is filled with challenges.

Challenge is part of farm life. Like in southern Minnesota, we brave snow, wind, and ice storms. We either have too much or too little water. The weather determines the crops we raise and the price we get. We have faced the weather challenge often.

Our garage covered with tent caterpillars
Note all the bare trees in the background.

But in the summer of 2001, we faced a new challenge--an infestation of tent caterpillars. They started slowly after a late spring. We noticed a few, and before we knew it the landscape was alive with crawling critters.

We tried remedies like spraying a mixture of Dawn detergent and water around trees, but it soon became apparent we were fighting a losing battle.

They were everywhere--on car tires, in our hair, on our shoes, on the sides of buildings and crawling up pants legs. From trees, bushes, and flowers they stripped off all the leaves that we had waited through a long winter to see, and by July 4, the landscape was brown. When the caterpillars finally crawled into their cocoons, the rains came and flooded the land.

We hoped to recover from lost crops, but then came the big flood of 2002. With bridges down and land under water, it was impossible to move machinery. Some quit farming, but we stayed and kept the faith. As the eternal optimists, we found jobs to supplement, looked forward to better times, and adjusted our spending habits.

We don't need to go to the nearby casino to gamble; everyday life is a gamble. Yet we continue to live in the far north. People here are a tough breed that has weathered many storms. And they are wonderful. The community reaches out generously with time and money and pulls together to face each new crisis.

In response to a high number of traffic accidents involving local youth driving to other towns for entertainment, community members organized forces, conducted fund raisers, and built a community-owned movie theater that shows recently released films. Kids and adults now have a nice place to go without having to drive on dangerous roads late at night. Baudette folks saw a problem and took steps to find a solution. Baudette is that kind of town.

So we remain here in Baudette. All four kids graduated from high school here, and two got married in this town. Two of our children went away to college and returned. Two live three hours out of the area but are looking to return. I still say, when we are planning a trip to Albert Lea, that we are going down home. But despite the hardships and the challenges, I think we made the right move when we came to Baudette.

Carol Adair Brune graduated from Albert Lea High School in 1964 and Naeve Hospital School of Nursing. She enjoys her children and grandchildren , along with various community activities.

CTC--It's a Theater
by Jennifer Laura Paige

Part I: A Big Sign

I was wearing a floor length muslin rehearsal skirt, which I constantly tripped over; under that, I was wearing ripped jeans, clunky winter boots, and a quilted plaid flannel vest. Someone had folded a piece off a white drop cloth and draped it over my head, in a loose attempt to signify a wedding veil. My groom was wearing jeans and a sweater. We stood staring stupidly at each other, as hordes of small children in kerchiefs and yarmulkes chased each other around the room, pausing occasionally to feed their virtual pets.

The director and the playwright were engaged in a heated debate. The cast had started blocking this sequence at ten in the morning, attempting to faithfully recreate the intricacies of a traditional Jewish wedding ceremony. It was now 1 p.m., and the last run-through of this sequence had taken nearly five minutes. Five minutes may not sound like a long time, but to a company of actors whose audience was going to consist primarily of middle school children, five minutes onstage with no dialogue and no plot development felt like an eternity.

The director wondered aloud whether there was anything we could do to make the ceremony shorter. "Does she have to walk around him seven times?" he asks, pointing at me. "What about three times? Won't they get the general idea?"

The playwright, a lovely woman whose dedication to telling the story of her ancestors' immigration to America from the shtetles of Russia had been unwavering, began to waver. "I just don't know...," she said cautiously. "This is a very significant ritual --every step means something different. People will know if it isn't right. You can't just cut things out of it."

We tried it again, in hopes that more practice would tighten the pace. With my "veil" covering my face, I couldn't see anything, and nearly crashed into the rabbi. By the time my betrothed finally stomped down on the plastic cup beneath his foot, four and a half minutes had passed. It was a definite improvement, but still too long.

"I think what we have to do," said the director, " is show the spirit of the wedding ceremony without actually doing all of it. We can have them drink from the wine glass once—and that can symbolize all the other times." The playwright still wasn't sure we could do that. Although she was also beginning to realize that this sequence was taking up too much time, she didn't want us making a mockery of her heritage. So the playwright did what she had always done whenever questions of authenticity and tradition arose during rehearsal—she called her mom.

She returned a few minutes later, looking vastly relieved. "It's okay," she said cheerfully. "We don't have to show the entire ceremony. We can just--suggest." The director and assistant director huddled together and began figuring out what to cut.

"What the heck," the playwright said with a shrug. " It's a theater! People know it's a theater. And if they don't--we'll just put up a big sign that says 'It's a theater'."

I was immediately struck with an image of confused audience members who had wandered into their seats by mistake, perhaps en route to Cousin Ira's wedding.

"Where are we?" I imagined them whispering to themselves. "Is this a theater?" The fact that I was the bride in this wedding, and not supposed to laugh under any circumstances, made it nearly impossible for me to keep a straight face. For the first time all day, I was grateful that I had a blanket over my head.

It may appear as though I laughed out of disrespect for this playwright or the dilemmas that she faced when collaborating with others to bring a personal story alive on the stage, but in fact, I admired her very much, and still do. Although her remark still makes me laugh, I also find it to be very profound. Whenever I hear an actor, director or audience member balk about theatrical conventions that require a slight suspension of disbelief—casting actors who don't look alike as siblings, for example, or dressing the set of an ornate Southern mansion with battered props gathered from the Goodwill—things which, ultimately, are not as important to me as honest acting and good storytelling-- my standard reply remains, "It's a theater. Didn't you notice the big sign outside?"

Part II--A Day in the Life

Children's Theater Company occupies a big white building in South Minneapolis; on the outside of the building, there is, in fact, a very big, brightly colored sign proclaiming it to be a theater. As a child I often went to Children's Theater on school field trips, and with my family; as a child who loved being the center of attention, I desperately wanted to be onstage there myself. I finally got my wish as an adult after I auditioned to be a performing apprentice for one season of shows. Performing apprentices received stipends of $150 a week. I had just turned 20 years old, and had never had a full time job before, so this actually sounded like a reasonable amount of money to me.

My day began with an 8 a.m. ballet class, followed by a group warm-up session for a 10 a.m. student matinee. I shared a big, group dressing room with two other female apprentices and ten or fifteen child actresses between the ages of 8 and 18. After the school show was over, I sometimes spent a few hours rehearsing the current "apprentice project"— usually a small studio production of a Shakespeare or Chekhov play, undertaken to keep our dramatic skills sharp after several months of wearing animal costumes and speaking in couplets.

I sometimes had an afternoon rehearsal for the next show in the season, an understudy rehearsal, or a costume fitting. If I had a few hours off, I often stopped by the accounting office and stuffed envelopes for $5 an hour.

I almost never went home—in part, because it was a brutal winter that year, and I didn't have a car. Mostly though, it was a deliberate choice--I wanted to spend all of my time at the theater. In the evening, I sometimes had another performance. In the fall and winter, when two shows were running simultaneously, I stayed after the show to help the crew change the set from one repertory show to the other. This was another opportunity the theater provided for the apprentices to make a little extra money.

I also picked up work shifts answering phones at the switchboard and moving scenery in and out of warehouses. I helped direct traffic at children's auditions. My entire life revolved around the theater. Although

I had participated in theater since I'd been a small child, this year provided me with my first true understanding of what it means to live an artistic life. I began to think of the theater as a living organism

Part III--Inventory

During that year when I was a performing apprentice, I played a slang-talking teenage babysitter who talked on the phone incessantly, failing to notice that the kids had been absconded to Mother Goose Land.

I played a singing Dr. Seuss character, wearing an enormous foam pod, an outrageous orange wig, a latex nose, and makeup that rendered me completely unrecognizable to all of my friends and relatives who came to see the show. I played the petulant young bride in a play based on a story by Sholom Aleichem.

Although I took three years of high school French, the only French phrases I remember how to say correctly are " Madame! Voici un petit elephant!" and " Bonne nuit, Babar, et fait du beau reves--" my only two lines as Monique, the French maid, in *The Story of Babar.*

I came back on stage after some performances to help answer questions from children who wanted to know the secrets behind all the stage magic. I understudied both a 40-year-old woman and a 12-year-old girl, and worked in nearly every department of the theater. My group of apprentices also performed black box productions of a Shakespeare piece, a contemporary absurdist comedy, and an experimental play based on a Chekhov short story.

Jennifer Paige as the babysitter in Tomie dePaolo's "Mother Goose" at CTC, 1995.

I appeared in over 300 individual performances of seven different shows. I helped to reenact the numerous hardships that the playwright's ancestors, and others like them, endured on their long journey to America.

Standing on the deck of a boat, I saw the Statue of Liberty emerging in the distance. I pointed it out to the actress playing my sister; we embraced, and waved ebulliently with our hankies as music swelled throughout the auditorium. Many of my cynical, jaded, twenty-something friends sheepishly admitted to weeping openly during this sequence, and I didn't doubt it. The stories and images that move us as children remain and will always remain a part of us. The power of simplicity is undeniable.

Jennifer Laura Paige was born in Golden Valley and moved to California at age 11. After graduating from the Los Angeles County High School for the Arts, she returned to her home state and graduated from the University of Minnesota. She is an actor, writer, and playwright who works in Minneapolis and St. Paul.

From the Inaugural Address to the People of Minnesota
by Governor Tim Pawlenty

A few weeks after I was born, a young president stood in the bright sunshine of a Washington January afternoon and said these words: "Let the word go forth from this time and place, to friend and foe alike, that the torch has been passed to a new generation of Americans."

Today a new generation of Minnesotans accepts the torch of leadership. Through the grace of God and the diligence of our people, we'll accomplish what each generation in turn strived to accomplish: to carry the torch higher, further and more boldly. We begin the challenge ever mindful of the sacrifices made by the generations that came before us. We stand on their shoulders and we thank them.

A few years ago, Tom Brokaw wrote *The Greatest Generation*. It's the story of my parents' generation. A few decades ago, my mom died. A few years ago, my dad died. A few days ago, my father-in-law passed away. The circle of life is soon going to be complete for that generation.

As the torch is passed from my parents' generation to mine and soon to the next, it's our duty to pass on their story and their principles. Many parents and others in that generation grew up in the Depression. As young adults, they went off to fight wars, and they literally kept the world free. They came back from wars and built much of the infrastructure of this country: schools and highways and freeways and technology that we're still benefitting from.

They faced enormous challenges. They didn't flinch. They didn't complain. They didn't blame someone else. They worked hard, and they faced their problems head on. They made enormous sacrifices. They did it because, like generations before them, they knew this fundamental truth: America is not great because we are smarter than the rest of the world. America is great because average people, like you and me, have enjoyed more freedoms and more liberties than any people that have ever lived. That spirit is alive and well in our great home state. Minnesota is not defined by boundaries on a map, but by our beautiful, bountiful land, our indomitable people, and a tremendous spirit of innovation that is the Minnesota Way.

We are blessed with fifty-four million acres of softly rolling plains, thick pine forests, rugged river bluffs and placid lakes disturbed only by the call of the loon.   From the solitude and freedom of our wide-open spaces to productive farm fields to our bustling cities and communities, we're a great state made even greater by our people. God gave us each freedom and nearly limitless opportunity.   These gifts have been the foundation for a spirit of innovation unmatched in all the world.

Minnesota is great because we build great progress out of great challenges.   We always have and we always will. The people of Rochester suffered a devastating tornado.   The solution was to create what became the Mayo Clinic.   Decades ago, thousands here and around the world suffered from the crippling effects of polio.   The Minnesota solution was the Sister Kenny Institute and what became Abbott Northwestern Hospital.

In Little Falls, a kid who felt isolated and hemmed in found the courage and the know-how to be the first person to fly an airplane across the Atlantic Ocean.

Twenty years ago, when we had too much corn and too much air pollution, the Minnesota solution was ethanol.   Our winters are too long and sometimes we didn't have enough to do so the Minnesota solution was to build snowmobiles.   Our houses in the winter were too cold or too hot, so Minnesotans invented the thermostat.   Years ago, a bad heart too often meant the end of life.   Minnesotans invented cardiac pacemakers and implantable defibrillators.

Iron ore in the Mesabi and Vermillion ranges helped win two world wars.   When those deposits were depleted, Minnesotans perfected new methods to mine and process taconite that kept a vital industry alive.   When people were starving in India, University trained scientists invented new hybrids that started the Green Revolution for that country and elsewhere.

I could go on talking about Scotch Tape, water skis, Post-it notes, Sears and Roebuck, the Pillsbury Doughboy, Greyhound Bus Lines, Meals on Wheels, the group medical practice and even our beloved Spam. Minnesota has made the world a much better place because the world gave us problems and we gave it progress.

With pride in our heritage and hope for the future, let us do the work entrusted to us and carry the torch of the future higher, more boldly and farther than ever before--all of us together, as Minnesotans. It is not a single torch that passes today. It's a light that passes from candle to candle until we have lit our whole wonderful state with hope, opportunity, and a new vision.

Thank you. May God bless the great State of Minnesota.

Tim Pawlenty grew up in South St. Paul and earned undergraduate and law degrees from the University of Minnesota. He was a member of the state House of Representatives for ten years before becoming Minnesota's 39th governor in 2003. He and his wife Mary have two daughters.

**Minnesota Memories 3 stories
came from these towns and cities.**

Map courtesy of Minnesota Office of Tourism

If you enjoyed reading *Minnesota Memories 3,* tell a friend and share the fun. This book and the original *Minnesota Memories* and *Minnesota Memories 2* are available at most major book stores, many gift shops, by direct mail, on Amazon.com and at public libraries.

If you have a story you'd like to submit for the next volume, send it to the address printed below. I don't mind a few misspelled words or dangling participles. A good story is a good story, and if your story is good, I'll try to polish it up and put it in the next volume. An overwhelming response from storytellers all over Minnesota suggests that many more stories should be published in many more volumes. Here's your chance to become part of recorded history. I look forward to hearing from you.

Joan Claire Graham
Purveyor of Memories

Storytellers may submit true stories for *Minnesota Memories 4* to the address below. Inquiries about book talks and presentations at stores, organizations, historical societies, libraries, classes, reunions, get-togethers or events are also welcome.

Need a gift? We'll include gift wrap and a card.
To order *Minnesota Memories* or *Minnesota Memories 2*, send
$13.95 plus $3 postage & handling
Minnesota Memories
11505 Monongahela Drive
Rockville, Maryland 20852
Phone: 301-770-1259
Email: MinnMemory@aol.com
(no spaces between words or letters in email address)
****
Special Offer: *Minnesota Memories Minnesota Memories 2*
$25 for both, postage included--Save $9!
3-Book Set*: Minnesota Memories, Minnesota Memories 2*
& *Minnesota Memories 3*--$36 for All 3! Postage Included-Save $15
Cash, checks to Minnesota Memories, or money orders accepted
Mention this coupon when you order.